JOHN A. COOK, A FORMER BANK VICE-PRESIDENT
HAS COME OVER TO *YOUR* SIDE.

WITH HIS IN-DEPTH EXPERIENCE AND INVESTMENT
ADVICE, YOU CAN ACQUIRE THE CONFIDENCE AND
KNOWLEDGE YOU NEED TO FIGHT BACK AGAINST
BANK INTIMIDATION—AND WIN!

"You do have a choice. You can get real service from
your bank if you know how to do it. By the end of this
book you will. How you change your whole relationship
with your bank is not a matter of magic or tricks. It will
evolve through a real understanding of who they are,
why they abuse you the way they do, and how you can
take the insider's view I'm going to share with you, and
turn it to your great advantage. Once you understand
your enemy, and how they think and work, you can
beat them at their own game."

—JOHN A. COOK

"I CAN THINK OF NO BETTER BOOK THAT EX-
PLAINS HOW BANKS WORK, HOW THEY DON'T
WORK, AND WHAT YOU CAN DO WHEN THEY
ARE WORKING AGAINST YOU."

—BERNARD MELTZER

All You Need To Know About Banks

John A. Cook & Robert Wool

BANTAM BOOKS
TORONTO · NEW YORK · LONDON · SYDNEY

Library of Congress Cataloging in Publication Data

Cook, John A. (John Andrew), 1943-
All you need to know about banks.

"A Robert Wool book"—T.p. verso.
Includes index.
1. Banks and banking.   2. Bank loans.   3. Credit.
I. Wool, Robert, 1934- . II. Title.
HG1601.C757 1983 332.1 82-90331
ISBN 0-553-23915-5

To Mom
J.A.C.

Again, to Bridget, and this time to Vanessa, also
R.W.

Acknowledgments

To Jack Romanos, Linda Grey, and Linda Cunningham, who have been so supportive, and whose keen editorial judgment contributed so fully to this book.

To Natalie Zabrocky, whose research and general assistance meant so much to us.

And to our many friends and former colleagues in the banking world who gave us their time, their knowledge, their best advice.

J.A.C. and R.W.

Contents

Chapter 1

Why they make
you feel so bad

You've had it with your bank.

First, they bounced a check on you, even though by all reasonable standards and your careful arithmetic, you had deposits in there to cover it.

Then, they made a mistake, which they acknowledged, sort of, but that they can't seem to clear up: They charged your account for a $50 withdrawal made by someone with a name spelled like yours. That was three months ago, and it still hasn't been straightened out.

A few weeks ago, when you went in to find out about their new Super Silver Checking, which apparently would pay you interest on your checking account balance, the bank officer the guard led you to for information wasn't exactly rude, but he certainly made you feel as if you were wasting his valuable time.

This, in addition to the usual abuse, of course. In addition to the eternal lines. In addition to the general unpleasantness of the tellers.

The last straw was yesterday. Trying to make absolutely

sure you would not bounce another check, you wanted them to give you immediate clearance on a check you had from the U.S. government. It was a refund on your federal income tax, a beautiful green check from the U.S. Treasury Department in the amount of $1,183.78. You were planning to use part of it for next week's vacation and wanted to buy some travelers checks.

You waited for one of the three pale men in the dark suits sitting on the platform to be free, then told him your problem.

"Sorry," he said, "can't help you."

"But surely you know this check is good."

He turned it over in his hands. "Perhaps it is," he allowed. "Even so. If we give you this money today, we'll be making an interest-free loan to you until we can collect the funds from the government. If we make an interest-free loan to you, have to make them to everyone. That would put us out of business."

It was one of those moments when you were so staggered by the ridiculousness and stupidity of what was said, you were speechless. You were also so outraged that you knew you'd better stay silent. Any words out of your mouth would probably get you shot by the guard.

You fumed over that insult for the rest of the afternoon. And then you had your moment of clarity.

"What's wrong with me?" you said to yourself. "They don't want my business. It's as simple as that, isn't it? They give me lousy service, make mistakes, are rude, and then when I ask them for a small favor, they tell me to get lost.

"Well, fine, then. They're not the only bank in town, not even the only bank on the block. I'm going down the street to First Consolidated."

And so you do. You've seen a number of their ads recently on television and in the paper. They seem to have all the latest kinds of accounts—Golden Egg Savings and Super Money Checking, they call theirs—and their ads all say: "At First Consolidated, a person gets treated like a person . . . not a number." That's all you're asking for.

Only a funny thing happens on the way to asserting your independence. You walk into First Consolidated, and immediately you see that their lines are even worse than the ones you left behind.

Then, you start to look around for some of those friendly faces you saw in the TV ads, but instead of finding those warm human beings, you find the same sour-looking men and women at the same paneled desks you left behind.

A guard does you a favor and guides you to an officer, and before you are barely in the seat by her desk, she's asked you two questions that are not friendly. Instead of explaining to you the differences among their various accounts, she simply wants to know: How much is your initial deposit? And, what's your anticipated average monthly balance going to be in the account?

Your palms grow moist, and you have a sinking feeling in your heart. You hand over the check from the feds for $1,183.78 and tell her you're really not sure of what your average monthly balance will be.

"Fine," she says. "What you want is a special Checking Account. They're handled downstairs."

She gives you back your check, puts away the New Account cards she had pulled from her drawer, turns her back on you, and picks up her phone.

You rise slowly, once again stunned by the sharp indifference and natural surliness of a bank officer.

The question in your mind is a fair one: Do I have any choice? Or, if I want to use a bank—and how else can I handle my affairs—must I suffer the same abuse from every single bank? Should I go downstairs to the pits where this dreadful woman has just shunted me, open the damned account and shrug it off—just another bit of insult and degradation that's part of our everyday life? Or, is there some other way?

For more than fifteen years, I was an officer with The Bank of New York, and for several of those years, I was that guy in the dark suit the guard led you to. I like to think I was different from what I've just described, which is, unfortunately, the kind of man or woman and the kind of service you will encounter in banks all over America today.

That is not to say there is no hope. You do have a choice. You can get real service from your bank, actually be treated like a human being, if you know how to do it. By the end of this book, you will.

How you change your whole relationship with your bank is not a matter of magic or tricks. It will evolve through a real understanding of who they are, why they abuse you the way they do, and how you can take the insider's view and knowledge that I'm going to share with you and turn it to your great advantage. Once you understand the enemy, and how they think and work, you can beat them at their own game.

Let's start with what I call The Consumer Paradoxes.

You are the consumer, and from time to time, you wonder if your bank really cares at all about your business. You have a checking account, a small savings account, and it seems that they couldn't care less, as you're reminded every time you step into their money shrine.

Paradox Number 1: They need you, but it kills them to admit it.

They need volume. They need your account and hundreds of thousands like it. The Bank of America maintains more than three million personal checking and savings accounts, and that's one big reason why they are the largest bank in North America.

However, the tradition of banking is something else. It is not to serve the masses, the man and woman in the street. The tradition of banking is founded on rich people, gentlemen with the right accents from the right schools providing financial services to rich people, many of whom have the same right accents, went to the same right schools.

It is very tough for bankers to face the change. Even though the "retail" side of banking is essential to nearly every commercial bank in the country, it is still looked down upon. The hotshot out of Stanford Business School who goes into banking today certainly has no interest in "retail." He wants "corporate," where he can make those big loan deals with major corporations and get involved in concocting complicated financial structures.

Paradox Number 2: Even though a bank knows it wants "retail" volume and knows it should advertise in such a way to attract it—"You're never just a number, you're a person . . ."—that bank also knows that personal service takes time, and time is money.

The Bank of New York is a bank that still believes in giving personal service. Yet, many of us had superiors on our backs because they thought we were spending too much time on customers' problems, not enough time, say, bringing in new business. A bank officer's time is money, which is one of the reasons your bank takes over three months to straighten out that $50 error they made against your account.

Paradox Number 3: The traditional banker's image might make you trust him with your money, but it leads to aloofness.

The distinguished gray-haired WASP (White Anglo-Saxon Protestant) in the conservative suit. That is the main-line tradition of banking. Even today, if you look at the heads of the ten largest banks in America, probably eight out of these ten will be men with model WASP credentials. And they will look it.

In the world of banking, appearances matter enormously. The traditional image, bankers believe, engenders your confidence in them. You don't want a rock star in charge of your life's savings; you want someone who reminds you of the British foreign secretary, or at the very least, George Bush.

Even though banks are changing, traditions and WASPs die hard. The bank officer on the floor of your branch might not have the right family background, the right religion, the right schools. But, as we'll see later in this book, he or she knows what's expected of him by the top officers of the bank. They are expected to look, act, even talk like those top officers. A kind of supply-side WASPness, seeping down from the top. That bank officer knows that if he doesn't maintain the image of the great tradition, he simply isn't going to fit in. If he doesn't look and act like, well, a banker, he's not going very far in that bank. And, unfortunately for you, two of the qualities that seep down from the top are reserve and aloofness, or as some say, iciness.

Paradox Number 4: The conservative banker vs. the uncontrolled flood of "strangers."

People are attracted to banking as a profession for any number of good reasons that usually have to do with handling and making money and never have to do with giving service to people. They don't want to be social workers or doctors or salesmen. Their interests and personalities lie elsewhere. They are, for the most part, rather like their image—reserved, withdrawn, orderly, conservative, desirous of a controlled, neat world. There are a lot of smart money and numbers people in banking and very few who are good in dealing with other people.

If they end up in "retail," it is for these quiet souls like being tossed onto a battlefield, for that's what the floor of a branch seems like to them. That's why those with seniority choose the desks that are the farthest away from the railing, the protective moat. Nobody wants to be on the front line, where you and hundreds like you can walk right up and ask a question or demand service.

Not only is the typical banker unsuited for such personal hand-to-hand, eye-to-eye contact, he or she is not merely supposed to survive out there. He or she is supposed to conduct business out there, with these masses of strangers.

Paradox Number 5: Make loans, lots of loans, but only good ones.

Your bank makes most of its money by lending money. That shell-shocked banker's job is to make loans. During normal times, he is exhorted by his boss and his branch manager to make those loans, make those loans. If he doesn't, he gets no salary increases, no job promotions.

At the same time, he is supposed to make only good loans. Bad ones, and he can lose his job altogether. He is trained to be skeptical and continually on guard against crooks. How is that frightened banker supposed to know a good risk from a bad one out of those swirling masses? Would you lend money to a complete stranger? (As we'll see in Chapters 4 and 5, you can solve this dilemma for your banker, and in doing so, a lot of your banking problems at the same time.)

A bank's only product

To me, the importance of being a human being while also being a bank officer was obvious. I'm not talking about social work; I'm talking good business.

Quite simply, two bits of reality were at the center of my view.

The first was that we didn't make things. Our only product was service.

The second was that basically all commercial banks are the same. In the next chapter, we'll look briefly at some of the federal and state regulations that apply to commercial banks. The practical effect is to leave them competing heavily for your business, without a dime's worth of difference among them. Bank X is not permitted, for example, to offer you higher interest on your checking or savings account balance than Bank Y. Bank X will confect an advertising campaign that will make it seem as if they give you higher interest and the moon, not to mention a toaster, if you open your account with them. But that's nonsense, and you should understand that it is nonsense and pay no attention to those ads, never mind be in the least bit tempted to shift your business.

Furthermore, you should understand that even though banks compete strenuously, they are copycats. If one bank in your city lowers its interest rate on loans by half a percent, you can be sure that before the day is out, all the other major banks will do the same thing. Or, if one of them comes up with a new piece of marketing—a Visa credit card for you, with no annual service fee if you open a Regular Checking Account with them—if the first bank is successful in its campaign and attracts a lot of new accounts, the others will rush to offer the same thing.

The only way a bank can separate itself from all its regulated competitors and copycats is by the service it offers you. No matter what the ads say, no matter what kinds of new accounts they seem to be offering, no matter how many portable radios and electric barbecue grills, the only real difference is service, which is why I'll spend a certain amount of time in this book telling you how to get it for yourself.

It seemed so obvious to me, as I said, and giving personal service was the natural way for me. It was one of my frustrations with banking as a profession that I could never work quite the way I wanted, or find much support, never mind enthusiasm for my ideas.

I certainly did not do badly in my career. But I increasingly found limitations, irritations. The personal service area was one problem.

Loans were another. As I said, when you're an officer on the floor of a bank, especially a competitive big-city bank, you must develop a volume of loans if you're going to get ahead.

I had volume, and think I was a good loan officer. People ask me if I felt good when I made a loan to someone who needed the money. Yes, but I never mistook my job for a charity. I was, in fact, quite sharp at sorting out the good risks from the bad ones, and my record showed it.

I was also good at understanding my customers' problems. Why they needed a loan; why they might have had some credit trouble in the past but could still handle the loan payments today; why a small businessman might be in some trouble today, and so need a cash injection, but have a bright picture for tomorrow.

In fact, I always tried to make my customers feel as though we were working together on their money problems, and if there were any way in the world that I could justify their loan and get the money for them, I would. And I meant it. I fought for countless borderline cases, and won. Not because I was softhearted. But because I was certain that these people were reasonable risks for the bank, that they would pay their loans back on time, and that giving them the loans would only make them feel better about our bank and cause them to give us more and more business as time went by.

I was rarely wrong. Not only that, I felt I was doing my job: I was making good loans, increasing the volume on my record, and I got raises and promotions because of it. That's what I was also after, getting ahead.

Beware, the loan salesman

There was one aspect of the loan business I did not like, and it is something that has become extremely widespread in the banking business all over America. Enticement.

As I said, banks make most of their money by lending you money and charging you interest on that loan. So, the more they lend, the more they make, assuming of course that you pay them back. What this leads to is ad campaigns designed to entice you into borrowing money, even if you don't really need it or can't afford it.

Imagine that the bank floor is an automobile showroom,

and your bank officer is a car salesman. You walk in to look over a new model you've seen advertised on your TV screen. That salesman has only one thing in mind, to sell you the car and as many accessories as he can.

The suit, accent, and style might differ, but that's what bankers are turning into. The car salesman couldn't care less that you have no business spending $10,000 for a car. So long as you pass their minimal credit checks, he's going to sell you that vehicle. Believe it or not, your bank officer is doing the same thing. His credit requirements on a $10,000 loan are more stringent, but basically he is selling you his product because that's what he's been hired to do. Do you really need that $10,000 loan? Could you get by with $5,000? Those are questions you had better ask yourself, because there are precious few loan officers today who care much about your interests.

It could be, of course, that I was never cut out for banking. I did well enough, but it's tough to move up in banks at a very rapid clip. With the exceptions of the Bank of America and Citibank, both notoriously fast tracks in the industry, banks resemble government bureaucracies when it comes to advancement. Jobs are extremely secure. As the saying in the industry goes, if they don't catch you stealing, you can stay for life. I reached the point where I was willing to trade the security for a chance to use my acquired knowledge of banking and finance to earn more than I was likely to ever earn from a bank. Opportunities presented themselves, and given my frustrations, here I am, looking at those people behind those desks in a completely new way.

It's not exactly from the same perspective you have. More like having a kind of super vision, being able to see from inside out and the other way around. That should help, as we go through this book.

Most of all, I want to take you where I've been, inside the bank, so you can understand the way things really work, how they perceive you, what they want out of you. Once you can share the insider's view, I think you'll be able to develop a completely new attitude toward your bank, and for the first time you'll be able to get your bank to work for you, instead of the other way around, which I am sure is the nature of your banking relationship today.

Let's start by looking at fears.

What is it about banks that makes people so afraid of them?

People have even asked me, if there is some invidious, subtle, secret campaign that banks wage to humble you. The answer is no, they don't have to. You go into your bank, and it happens: That cold feeling passes over you, even when you are giving them *your* money.

And when you are in there to ask for some of *their* money, absolute palpitations, tremors. I saw it with person after person who came to my desk for a loan.

The money commodity

To me, such a meeting was business as usual. To those people, to you, it is obviously something else. Let's explore that "something else," so that you'll be able to start doing business with your bank as nothing more or less than "business as usual" too.

Begin by thinking of money as your banker does—it is nothing but a commodity.

You go in for a loan carrying enormous amounts of emotional baggage on your back. For the banker, money is a commodity to be bought and sold. It has no more emotional content than, say, wheat, another commodity that is bought and sold.

If you were sitting at my desk in the bank trying to buy a shipment of wheat from me, all you'd be thinking about is the terms. You wouldn't have all those emotions tilting your mind.

You certainly, for example, wouldn't be worried about a personal rejection. Yet, you ask me for a loan of my money commodity, for which you're willing to pay me a fee called "interest," and immediately the words are out of your mouth, you are scared that you will not be given the loan, which will be a form of personal rejection. You won't be given the money because somehow you are not worthy. In fact, it is a set of numbers that provides the foundation for the bank's decision whether or not to make the loan. Will this loan be good business or bad business, I must ask myself. Has this person the income to pay us back?

Again, if we were talking about wheat, and we couldn't agree on terms, you wouldn't take it personally. You'd leave my desk thinking, I'd better go down the street and see if I can't get the wheat on better terms. Business as usual.

What they don't check

From my observation, the anxieties most people have about banks come in two shapes, free-floating and specific.

The specific ones are relatively simple. For example, the worries when you fill out a loan application. "Is my reason for the loan good enough?" you wonder. "And, here, where it asks me what I earn in a year, am I making enough?"

Understandable worries, and they deeply shake many people. In fact, let me share something with you that I could not when I was sitting at that desk. Important as those two pieces of data might be, as we'll see in Chapter 8 when we dissect the whole application, the bank never really knows whether your answers to those questions are true or not.

Surprising as it sounds, I'm sure, there is no way they can know what you are really going to do with the money they lend you.

And, when it comes to what you earn, in recent years larger banks have stopped checking. We'll see just how important that piece of information is in the formula your bank applies to decide how large a loan to give you. Yet the bank is going to take your word for what you put down. In almost all cases, they won't bother to call your employer to verify your salary.

Or, to take another specific anxiety, I've seen that women, blacks, old people, and other minorities tend to worry that banks will discriminate against them. To be sure, they have solid, historic reasons for that fear. I'll tell you quite a bit about the prejudices bankers do have, but we'll also see how the law protects you from many of those discriminatory attitudes and how you can deal with them yourself, directly. No need to have such worries hovering over you.

Free-floating anxieties are a bit tougher to handle. The first of them is money itself. Another book could be written about the psychological effects of money. So many people can't handle it, get in trouble with it. I came to think that it has a lot to do with growing up. If you handle your money affairs, you are a grown-up. Avoid or mismanage your money affairs, you are still a little kid. Little kids aren't expected to handle their financial affairs. Lots of people don't want to grow up.

But I was a banker, not a psychiatrist. If it was clear to me that people asking for loans had not been able to manage their money, that they had a history of overdrawing their checking accounts, or their credit reports showed a string of accounts on which they were chronically late in paying bills, I didn't lend them money. Simple as that.

Taming the computer monster

In the area of loans, I found a widespread anxiety about computers. It was you against the computer, an all-knowing computer, and what chance could you possibly have to explain yourself to such a machine?

In fact, as we'll see in Chapter 9, there are a number of ways you can deal with your bank's computers, starting with the personal relationship you develop with your banker. Once you understand how the system works, where the computer comes into your banking life, I think you will see that particular fear dissolve. Which is what I hope we can do throughout this book: dispel mystery and, with it, dispel fears.

Like the scary notion that somehow, someone in the bank can punch the wrong button and wipe out your credit. People have told me they were worried that a teller was going to make a mistake, and suddenly, their balances would disappear; their credit would be ruined.

Well, tellers can and do make mistakes, usually minor matters quickly caught. Believe me when I tell you that tellers cannot punch some super button and erase you, cause you to become a nonperson in the bank.

Another area that alarms people is the whole business of credit, and understandably so. They are worried that lies and mistakes will find their way into those mysterious credit files. Once again, those villainous computers appear, storing away God knows what information on us all, data spewed forth when the bank wants to decide whether or not to let you have the money you desperately need and want.

I have more good news. In Chapter 7, we'll unravel the whole process, and you'll see that you can find out exactly what's in your credit report, and if there is anything erroneous, just how you can get it corrected. Or, if there is bad stuff in there that, alas, is accurate, how you can handle that information in your loan campaign, so it might not be very damaging at all.

There is one free-floater that affects practically everyone, the feeling of neglect and indifference, that so far as your bank is concerned, you are nothing but a number.

You are not imagining anything here. You are not being paranoid. The truth is that to them, you *are* nothing but a number. I've already suggested some of the reasons. They have to do with the tradition of banks to serve a handful of rich folks, not mobs of unknown people off the street; with the WASP sensibility; and with the kind of reserved people banks attract to work for them. Plus, of course, that numbers are much neater, cleaner, easier, and more economical to deal with than individuals.

Yet, as we'll see in Chapters 4 and 5, you can change all that, remove yourself from the faceless mob, and develop a personal relationship with your banker. Once you do that, you are no longer what he calls a "walk-in," one of the most damning labels in banking, nor are you a number. You are in his eyes just what you want to be, a regular human being who wants to be treated as such. And, believe it or not, that's just what he'll do for you. He'll give you service.

Chapter 2

How they make money and where you fit into their plans

The only person I ever met who felt sorry for banks was a real estate broker, a remarkably stupid real estate broker, who said to me during one of those periods when banks were making almost no mortgages: "I just don't know how banks make ends meet."

Banks are fairly mysterious businesses to most people. Over the years, the general impression I've gathered is that most people see us getting rich in a few ways. First, we charge them every month for our services, and we charge them interest on the loans we make. That stuff is clear and simple. Beyond that, they imagine we are making millions in the stock market and buying up whatever we want all over the universe. These last two activities are funded rather magically. Partly from all the millions we somehow accumulate, and partly from those machines we have down in the vaults that make money.

Not very accurate, but in fact there is magic in our

business process. There is, what I call, completely
legal alchemy going on, and this is the way it works.

Today, you and 999 people like you deposit in your
bank an average of $500 each. Frankly, your $500 alone
is not so exciting to them, but as a group you people
represent $500,000. Half a million dollars is interesting.
And that, thanks to the legal magic, is only the beginning.

In the name of relative safety, banks are required by
law and regulation to keep a portion of your $500, and
that collective $500,000, readily available. After all, you
might deposit $500 today and want to withdraw it
tomorrow, and if so, the money should be available.

So, the Federal Reserve Bank tells them they must
keep a percentage of the deposits they receive in
reserve. That percentage, the "reserve requirement,"
varies, depending on the size of the bank, the type of
deposit, and the amount of money the bank has in those
deposits. Also, the Fed sets it on something of a graduated scale. So, with what are called "Transaction Accounts,"
which includes your checking account, the Fed says,
keep in reserve 3 percent of the first $25 million that's
deposited with you, plus 12 percent of everything
over $25 million. Either keep it in cash in your own
vaults, or make a deposit with us, the Federal Reserve
Bank.

The reserve requirement changes from time to time,
according to the policies and objectives of the Fed. If
they, for example, want to see less money floating
around the economy, they can increase the reserve
requirement and take that much more money out of
circulation.

But whatever the actual reserve requirement might
be, it leaves your bank with the balance of your deposit.
If the requirement amounts to 15 percent, your bank
must keep 15 cents of every dollar around in cash. That
leaves them with 85 cents of your dollar to work with.
Thanks to other regulations, they are not free to do
anything they please with that 85 cents, or $425,000 if
we consider your $500,000 aggregate. But one thing

they are free to do with it is lend it out, and that is one powerful freedom.

From your money, more money and profits

They are free, in other words, to create money, 85 cents worth of money from each of your dollars. When you deposit $500, you are creating for them, giving them the chance to create $425 to lend to someone else, at the going interest rate. That becomes $425,000, if we look at your group of depositors. The annual interest on $425,000 at, say, 15 percent is $63,750. Needless to say, even though it is your money that the bank is selling to make their $63,750, you don't get to share in the profit. It is theirs. That is how banks make the giant share of their money. And it is why they need you.

Your money is the cheapest money they can find. As we saw in the last chapter, money is a commodity. If they can't get it from you, they can go into the money market and buy it. They can buy it for short periods from other banks. They can buy it, in a manner of speaking, from the Federal Reserve Bank. But whenever they buy it, they are obviously cutting into their profit margin. And those margins are not huge. If a bank can realize a profit margin of about one-half percent on a corporate loan, it has done nicely.

On the other hand, if it can have its money supplied by you, and all it has to pay for the money are some services—checking and savings facilities, the personnel and computers to support them, the real estate to house them—their profit margin will be biggest of all.

Banks also make money by charging fees for handling trusts and investment portfolios for rich folk. I did that work for several years at The Bank of New York, which, along with Morgan Guaranty, had the best trust reputation in the U.S. We earned our fees, I think, and overall contributed a fair percentage to the bank's earnings.

But that was unusual. Normally, trust departments are loss leaders. They are conveniences concocted for rich folk, just so they won't feel the need to take their banking anywhere else.

Look at the annual report, the very expensive annual report of your own commercial bank, and what you'll see, along with all the nonsense about "stewardship in trying times" and the stiffest portraits this side of the nineteenth century, is that the vast share of their earnings typically come from loans, a small percentage from trust and management fees, almost all the rest from investments the bank itself has made.

Those investments are not millions tossed after the latest fad growth stock in the market. Those investments are carefully regulated. The U.S. government and usually your state government want your bank to be stable, so they tell them, you have money from depositors, invest in government bonds. And they tell them exactly what percent of those investments must be in federal bonds, what percent in state and local.

There are also common stocks in your bank's portfolio, but essentially they do not approach their investments as you might—to make a killing. They balance their investments, always in terms of their reserve requirements, and to keep themselves as liquid as possible. These investments, after all, are a primary source of new funds if they decide they want to increase the number of loans they're making.

Banks have hard times, too

While banks always want to lend money, there are times when they have to restrict their lending for good business reasons.

Not long ago, as my perceptive real estate broker observed, banks practically stopped making loans for mortgages. State laws prohibited them from charging more than around 12 percent, but it was costing the banks about 15 percent to buy their money. The state laws were relics of another era, when 12 percent was an enormously high rate and legislators were concerned that banks would get so greedy that good citizens and voters wouldn't be able to pay for mortgages and buy their own homes. So, they put a ceiling on what the banks could charge for mortgages.

When the cost of money got so high that the banks would be losing money on each mortgage loan, the banks said: "This is no way to do business. No more mortgage loans. If you want a different kind of loan, however, where there are no legislative ceilings, be our guest."

State legislatures then lifted their mortgage ceilings and the rates floated up, determined by the usual factors of the market, like supply, demand, and competition. If you wanted a mortgage, you had to pay the once unthinkable amount of 15 percent to 20 percent, but at least the money was available, if you were willing to pay. If you thought those rates were larcenous, there was no law requiring you to buy a house at that time and pay that kind of interest. Which, of course, is what millions of people said and did: They decided to wait, and the housing industry suffered a massive collapse.

There are other times when banks can hardly give their money away. I remember well the recession days of 1974–75. No one wanted to borrow.

Manufacturers, for example, looked at their sales figures and saw drops of 25 percent, 30 percent. No time to expand now, they said; no time to borrow money to build that new plant. Let's tighten our belts, hold on, and do what we can until the national economy changes and people have money to buy our product.

Individuals thought the same way. People were being laid off. No time to borrow money. That extension on the house can wait and so, certainly, can the dream vacation in Hawaii.

It was a crazy time in the bank. We had meeting after

meeting at which we were reminded of our purpose in life: "Gentlemen, the reason we are in business is to make loans. The reason you have your jobs, gentlemen, is to make loans."

We had actual pep talks. "You've got to think, breathe, eat, sleep, and dream of nothing but The Bank of New York. I want you to get out there and sell, sell, sell."

I remember after that particular rally that I couldn't resist going over to a friend and putting my head down on his desk. "What the hell are you doing, Cook?"

"Dreaming of The Bank of New York," I replied, "dreaming of The Bank of New York."

We were given goals for new accounts, deposits, loans, and they were tightly reviewed every month, and when you had fallen far below your quotas, you were spoken to in very unbankerly terms.

Then the most unbankerly measure of all was applied. We were ordered to make "cold calls."

"Cold calls" are just what they suggest: Without any introduction, you make a call on someone, walk into some office, cold, and try to sell them on doing their banking with you and borrowing money from you.

Banks all over New York were in the same state and trying the same desperate technique. We were supposed to make five "cold calls" a day, and every banker doing it was completely unsuited by temperament and training for the job. It was ridiculous, actually, all of us scanning the directories of office buildings, picking victims, all of us in our banker's suits knocking on office doors, forcing smiles, trying to get past wary receptionists who knew how to cope with stationery salesmen, and Xerox salesmen, and insurance salesmen, but who never had been confronted by a nervous banker claiming he just wanted to say hello and tell the boss about the wonderful services his bank was offering. When we first started our campaign, I encountered total incredulity. Even when I gave the receptionist my card, or sneaked my way past her to one of her bosses, they were absolutely disbelieving. And New York being New York,

I'm surprised no one called the cops to report a crazy person or a rapist impersonating a vice-president of a bank.

After a while, of course, they had so many of us coming around, that even though they weren't interested in buying our wondrous services, they at least knew we weren't dangerous.

After months and months of "cold calls," I had not made one single sale. I had, however, compiled a massive file of extremely optimistic Call Reports and another full of copies of letters to every regular customer I had, letters about nothing really, but which served as reminders that we were there and would be simply delighted to practically give them money.

Perhaps my most positive act during that rough time was keeping all my customers. Gentlemen bankers, I assure you, can be extremely competitive, and I had to fend off some sly maneuvers on the part of colleagues in my own branch to filch some customers, as well as other attempts by officers in other branches.

Regulations, and how they affect what you can get

Banking is the most regulated business in America. Exactly how, which is to say how the complicated banking system in America works, is not the point of this book. But there are aspects of the system worth looking at because they directly affect what your bank is allowed and not allowed to offer you and do for you.

The complex of regulating agencies is composed of federal and state organizations, implementing both federal and state laws. They cover absolutely everything a bank does from the hours it may stay open and days of the week it may do business, to the amount of interest it may pay on accounts, and the reserve requirements. They police and audit your bank, and they insure your deposits in it for up to $100,000.

This is true, whether you use a commercial bank, a

savings bank, or a savings and loan association. Commercial banks, like my Bank of New York, are the largest in North America. Ours was started by Alexander Hamilton, among others, and its purpose was mercantile. Commercial banks today are still the banks that business uses, and their primary services to individuals are checking and loans. Savings banks, on the other hand, were begun early in the nineteenth century to give common people a safe place to keep their money and to provide communities a source of capital to build homes. Personal savings accounts and mortgages have remained the traditional focus of savings banks, though that is changing, as savings banks struggle to compete with commercial banks and stay alive. Savings and loan associations, started in the 1830s, were first called "building and loan" associations, with people becoming members and pooling their money so they could have enough to build their own homes. Still largely mutually owned, savings and loans are very similar in tradition and service to savings banks.

The new banking legislation passed by Congress in October 1982, as this book was going to press, will allow thrift institutions for the first time to make a certain amount of commercial and business loans. Presumably, this will enable them to be more competitive with commercial banks, assuming of course, they make good loans. They will be entering an area where they have no experience, but if they are able to make the transition, they might indeed compete with smaller commercial banks. It is hard to envision any savings banks successfully competing in the area of business and commercial loans with any of the giant commercial banks.

Basically, of course, all the rules and regulations that control these banks are intended to protect you and your money. They have an additional effect, however, quite important for you to understand: They render all banks essentially the same.

Take the amount of interest your bank pays you. People would actually berate me because we didn't pay them more interest on their savings accounts. They called me a bandit. I told them the truth, and they never believed me, of course, because the truth was that the government wouldn't let us pay them a penny more. If the rate was then 5 percent, that was the maximum that we or any other commercial bank was allowed to pay.

They practically laughed at me when I told them that bankers wished they could pay more interest, be able to negotiate the rate, use it as a way to attract business.

Nothing could have been truer in recent years, when banks were prohibited from running their own money market funds and also prohibited from raising their interest rates to compete with the existing funds.

The funds were draining the banks, especially savings accounts, of billions. After all, no matter what we bankers told our customers, the truth was, that except for maintaining minimal amounts in savings—and even that was debatable—there were no rational reasons for them to keep their money in a savings account where it earned only 5¼ percent or 5½ percent, when a money market fund would pay them 12 percent to 15 percent.

Finally, last October, after a long and massive campaign by a frightened but wily banking industry, Congress gave commercial banks, savings banks, and savings and loan associations the right to offer accounts that are "directly equivalent to and competitive with money market funds."

And, these accounts will be insured up to $100,000 by the Federal Deposit Insurance Corporation (FDIC), or the Federal Savings and Loan Insurance Corporation (FSLIC). The money market funds had no such federal insurance, as banks kept reminding you day after day, even though the truth was that if you selected a conservative money market fund, one that put their money— and would be putting *your* money—into government paper, perhaps into bank CD's, perhaps into commercial paper, short-term loans to corporations with the highest credit ratings, you were pretty well insured by reality. I mean, if all those investments went bad, there'd be no America left, so federal insurance wouldn't do you much good anyway.

Of course, lots of people are less interested in reality than appearances, and federal insurance certainly appeared comforting, even though, in fact, those savings in those federally insured accounts were diminishing in real value daily because of inflation. Everything was insured all right but those poor souls were losing money, at a guaranteed annual rate. But illusions, habits, and fears die hard, as bankers know very well. If these good, honest Americans want to lose money by "saving" it in our banks, well, this is a free country. We're here to serve them. Be our guests. (More on this in Chapter 6.)

Because of other government regulations, I had other problems with people who were putting up stocks and bonds as collateral for a loan. They'd bring me stocks worth, say, $30,000, that they were going to let us hold against a loan of $30,000.

"I'm afraid we need more collateral," I had to tell them. "We can only figure this for seventy percent of the loan." That was the government margin requirement on common stocks, 70 percent. On government bonds, the margin was 90 percent. Over-the-counter stocks, more like 50 percent.

I'd explain all this, then tell them we needed another $9,000 in collateral on their $30,000 loan, and often, they'd try to negotiate with me. "I'm a good customer, surely you can do better than seventy percent for me." I had to give them a mini-course in the U.S. banking system before they'd believe me.

Regulations and competition

We end up with an odd situation. The regulations, as I noted, have the effect of leaving banks essentially the same in many key ways. The kinds of accounts, or limits on interest rates, or the margin requirements on loans, apply to all of the 15,000-plus banks in America.

At the same time, banks are very competitive. They have to be. But how? What can they offer you if they are all so regulated?

Much of it is junk. When the savings banks wanted to get around some of their regulations, they discovered premiums and gifts. You open a new account with a $1,000 balance, you get an electric blanket. Wait a minute; if those guys across the street give you an electric blanket, we'll give you that blanket *plus* a set of beer steins.

I had friends in those banks who, at first, were laughing themselves silly. People actually came in waving official checks from the bank across the street where they had just closed out their accounts, just to get their crummy gift.

They didn't laugh for long. Soon, those same customers were back, carrying their toaster, complaining that the thing was busted, and demanding that it be fixed immediately, or they'd withdraw all their money and go down the block where they could get a toaster *with a warranty*.

"I didn't know anymore if I was working in a bank, or Sears, Roebuck," one friend of mine told me. "We had all this junk piled up all over the place, people coming up to my desk to complain about electric can openers that didn't work, and a whole new set of security problems. It wasn't enough the guards were supposed to protect our money. Now they had to keep people from walking off with the sample appliances, and those people included our own employees."

That form of competition has nothing to do with banking. That belongs in the automobile showroom, and you should recognize it for that.

Banks also try to compete by giving the illusion of being different. "Put your money in our bank, and we'll pay you more interest," they seem to be promising. But, when you examine these offers closely, as we'll do in Chapter 6, you'll see that what they seem to be offering is not exactly what they deliver. They come up with alluring names for special kinds of savings accounts, for example, Golden Special, Super Golden Special, and in fact the thing will pay you not a measly 5½ percent interest, but 7½ percent, 8½ percent, maybe much more. But you've got to keep your money in that Super Duper Whopper for an agreed amount of time. If you need your money during that time, the bank might give it back to you, but with severe penalties. Not to mention that you might have put your money to much better use yourself over that period of time and earned yourself more money.

Quite simply, those are time deposits cloaked in fancy new duds. I have nothing against time deposits; I just don't like to see people turning their money over to banks without fully understanding what they're doing. But in fairness, when banks try to be competitive by pitching time deposits, at least they're still in the banking business, and not the appliance business.

A checking account is a checking account is a checking account

Speaking of fancy duds, banks bombard you with what appear to be countless forms of checking accounts, again the Golden this and Super that. Make life simple for yourself. No matter what they are called, there are only two kinds of checking accounts.

There is the Special Checking Account, where no minimum balance is required. Usually, you are charged for each check you write, and have monthly service charges in addition. They got their name in the mid 1940s, when banks began to widely open their checking facilities to common folk. The name "Special" obviously sounded good, and it was a way of setting these accounts off from the truly "special" accounts, which were confusingly called "Regular Checking."

Regular accounts were the accounts banks traditionally had with rich folk. There was regular business between bank and customer, a regular balance. Today, anyone who can maintain a minimum average balance, usually around $1,000, may have one. Some banks pay interest on your balance, over a certain amount; some eliminate monthly service fees in return for certain balances.

I don't believe those fringes are worth a moment's thought. Unless your balances are gigantic, what's the interest going to amount to? And there are so many more important considerations for choosing a bank than the few dollars you may or may not have to pay each month for checking services.

Between the two, it's much better to maintain a Regular Checking Account if you can sustain the average balance, though that's something else not to lose sleep over. Banks are much more concerned with your overall banking business than whether you meet their minimum balance each month.

The regular account does matter when it comes to credit. It tells the banker that you have certain means and your banking business is at a certain level.

Regular Checking Accounts, as we'll see, also can bring you extremely useful service from your banker. But Special Checking, contrary to the name, brings you nothing special.

And then there's competition that saves you money

Banks can also be competitive by offering you better terms. There certainly is no regulation that says all banks must charge you 16 percent interest on a mortgage loan, for example. A well-managed bank might be able to offer you a mortgage at 14 percent and still make money on that loan. Mortgages are a special breed of loan, as we'll see in Chapter 10, being for such large amounts, normally, and for such long periods of time. A difference of 2 percent in your mortgage rate could mean thousands of dollars to you over the life of that loan, so you must shop around before you sign up for one. When it comes to mortgages, you should think of banks, once again, as you think of car salesrooms. Compare prices and negotiate. This is an area where there is competition as you know it in the normal commercial world.

There is similar competition and the possibility of better terms with other loans. But except for car loans, it usually doesn't pay to shop around for the simple reason that most banks don't like to lend money to strangers. There are exceptions, which we'll consider, but for a personal loan, you will usually need some personal relationship with your banker or, at the least, some satisfactory banking association with the bank for a period of time. Car loans are different because on them the bank owns the car with you, which gives them fairly good protection on their loan, and bank requirements are looser on these loans. So, they are also definitely worth shopping around for.

The new banking legislation gives some promise of allowing greater true competition among banks, and better possibilities for consumers. I like the option of those high interest variable rate accounts, fully insured for $100,000. But the details and limitations of those and other elements of the bill are still being worked out, as this edition goes to press. So, I'll have to wait for a future edition to say much more.

There is one other area of competition in which banks are basically unregulated, and that can make an enormous difference to you. I'm talking again about service. As I said earlier, I always viewed that as our real product, and the way we could compete with other banks and win your business.

Throughout this book, I'll tell you what's available in your bank, or should be, and how you can get some for yourself. Service, as noted, costs the bank money, so they aren't quick to provide it for average customers. Better-than-average and what are called Preferred Customers are something else. But the rest of us have to push them for it. Believe me, it's worth doing. In the end, service is how you can tell one bank from another and how you can decide which bank to give your business to.

Perhaps now, you can begin to see that your business, modest as it might be, will matter to a bank. Looked at one way, you are lending them money that they can "recreate" many times over and lend to others for their own profit. They need you. With that in mind, don't let them treat you as if they were doing you a favor by permitting you to open an account with them.

Chapter 3

The making of
a banker

I went into banking for the same reason a lot of people do. I didn't know what I wanted to do once I had finished college. I had majored in Latin and Greek at Holy Cross, and I knew that wouldn't earn me much of a living. So I decided to go into business, of some sort.

Many of my friends, as indecisive as I, went to law school as a way of finding direction. I thought of that, even got accepted to New York University Law School, but decided I couldn't afford it. I was married, and we already had our first child, Deirdre. I had to earn money.

My choice of banking as a first step into the business world was not a bad one, and I find many college graduates still thinking in those same terms. In fact, it is a good graduate school of finance. What you learn, not only about banking but about investing, about managing money, about businesses large and small, is valuable to countless kinds of businesses.

Further, most banks will pay for you to go to graduate business school at night, which I did, so your credentials become extremely attractive to the business world.

In the course of your early years, you deal directly and indirectly with a great variety of businesses. The overview of business you get is wonderfully broad. Before long, if you want to leave the bank, often you can pick a company doing business with the bank and move to it.

Many people approach banking with just that in mind—use it as a starting point, an observation platform, and move on for the big corporate financial job. But many more never leave, whatever they had in mind at the start.

Working for a bank is seductive. It's so respectable, to start with. And with a few exceptions, the demands of the job are not that great, and the security is total.

Not everyone gets ahead, and banks are full of "lifers" who have been passed over time after time, year after year, fairly and unfairly. Banks take advantage of these people, knowing that after, say, fifteen years, they have no place else to go. So the banks benefit from their valuable experience, while keeping their salaries as low as possible.

Salaries in general are not high in banks. Tellers' salaries range from $160 to $180 a week to start, rise to about $225 after two to three years of loyal service. The lesser officers you see on the platform of your bank, the assistant vice-presidents who deal with people walking in to open small personal checking accounts, are paid $25,000 to $30,000.

The vice-presidents, sitting at the desks farther away from the railing, the ones who make the bigger consumer loans and deal with small businessmen, earn something in the area of $35,000 to $45,000.

The people you never see make the most, but even that isn't what their equals pull down in the outside world. The senior vice-presidents in charge of trusts, or corporate banking, or investing, all earn around $60,000 to $75,000.

The president of a medium-sized urban bank is paid $90,000 to $120,000, the chairman, $150,000 and up. In the very largest banks, the salaries rise to $150,000 and $250,000.

The people in the top positions of large banks are smart, tough, ambitious. But most people in banks are not. Most people with those characteristics leave banks pretty quickly. In fact, if they have those qualities, they aren't attracted to banks in the first place. They go directly to the hotter action and competition, and the bigger bucks. They go into business, or investment banking, or to some corner of Wall Street.

Banks attract people who are willing to trade big salaries for security and less pressure, though so-called "bankers hours" are a myth. Your bank might shut its tellers' windows and lock its main doors at three in the afternoon, but tellers are still there until five, doing their accounting of the day's business; and the officers, if they are serious about their careers, are there much, much later. I used to reach my desk about eight in the morning, conduct the normal business of the day until around three, then have personal meetings with customers late in the afternoon. I'd finish my paperwork and phoning between six and seven in the evening, and frequently meet a customer for dinner.

Big health and insurance plans, generous vacation schedules are common to banks. Loans are cheaper to employees. And as I said, don't steal and you can stay forever. Above all, you get to call yourself a banker.

That even meant a lot to me, at the beginning, and it absolutely paralyzed my family. Their son, the banker. My father had been killed in France in World War II, and my mother, who worked as a waitress to raise me, had married the bartender, a lovely man, who finally got a restaurant of his own. But we were living over a fruit store in Brooklyn when I started at the fancy Bank of New York, and it was pretty heady stuff.

The man who interviewed me for the job in 1965, and gave it to me, was an extremely sympathetic fellow, quite dapper and WASP-sounding, who surprised me by telling me that he was also Irish and Catholic. Things had certainly changed in The Bank of New York, he said, since the time he got out of Georgetown University and started here. People told him then he was crazy to work here. But he had done quite well, thank you, and he assured me, I would have even greater opportunity. He was honest with me, but still very proud of his company.

Trust us with your fortune

I decided to go into the Personal Trust Department, which is where we manage all those fortunes entrusted to us by rich folk.

The Bank of New York was noted for its trust department, and that appealed to me. But I also knew that most of the officers in the department were aging. Promotions can come very slowly in banks, so it made sense to me to pick a department where there would be openings before too long. Keep your mouth shut, your shoes shined, do your work, I told myself, and you'll move in this department. And I was right. By the time I was twenty-nine, I was a group head and a trust officer.

I started out low enough, wearing a frayed blue linen jacket and delivering mail to vice-presidents at their desks all over 48 Wall Street, our main office. It was a traditional, humbling beginner's job, carrying the mail to an officer, standing twenty feet from his desk, until he acknowledged my presence and beckoned me forward. After a week, fortunately, I was taken out of that demeaning role, and none too soon. There I was a college graduate, expected to behave like some clerk out of Dickens, and I was furious.

For about six weeks, I was moved through various departments—securities, estates, taxes, the vault—watching, not learning much, but getting some sense of what each department did and who the people were.

Then the real management training program started in trusts. Essentially, what we were doing was taking large sums of money and figuring out what to do with it, so it would work for people the way they wanted.

You inherit half-a-million dollars. You're not sure how to handle it; you come to us. We first try to figure out what your needs are so far as this money is concerned. Do you need the dividend income it could generate to live on? Maybe not. Maybe your kids will need it more than you. Maybe you don't need the money right now, but you will in fifteen years when you plan to retire.

Figuring out real wants and needs is never simple. People fool themselves, or they try to fool us. They don't want to admit to the enormously high scale they live on; it embarrasses them to be honest with us about it. You can spend a year meeting and talking with a client before you finally get the true picture.

Once you do, you create a portfolio to meet those needs. So much in common stocks, so much in bonds, this for real estate, that for options, a couple of Certificates of Deposit for $100,000 each where we lend the money to the bank for some months at a favored rate of interest.

Actually creating the portfolio is fairly simple. The tough work of tracking and selecting stocks, bonds, options, and the rest is done by various specialists within the bank. The trust officer makes his selections from the lists those specialists draw up of favored stocks, lists that are first approved by the bank's internal review committees.

At the beginning, I was really an administrative aide. I wrote up tickets for buying and selling, made sure that the money in our trust accounts was in balance, wrote the standard letters to clients to inform them that certain stocks had been bought for their accounts, that others had been sold. The most interesting part of the job was preparing for our monthly review sessions with the bank's Investment Committee.

In these meetings, every account we had was reviewed, and we had to be prepared to defend everything we had done with each account the previous month.

My job was to do the first review in preparation for the big meeting. I would look over each account in our group, see what the objectives of the account were, and make the first analysis of how we were doing and what kind of new action, if any, we should consider.

After about three years, I was made an assistant trust officer, with a management trainee of my own to do the grunt work. Now I was more involved in the actual shaping of the portfolios, and I began to meet our customers.

Then, three years later, I was promoted to trust officer, in charge of a group handling some 600 accounts, with four officers reporting to me.

The toughest part of the job, I quickly learned, was getting clients to make sense. It was their money, after all, and I had to make it work to serve their purposes. The problem was in getting them to realize what their needs really were, so we could handle their money in the way that was most advantageous to them.

If a man says to me, in effect, this is what I must have to live the way I now live, and I never want to wake up at three in the morning worrying about it, I can take it from there.

But it was never so simple. The young widow in New Jersey, for example, fell into a million dollars when her husband, who was thirty years older than she, died suddenly.

She summoned me to their mansion, soon after his death, and told me she wanted the whole thing invested in bonds. She needed the income she would get from the bonds to live in the style to which she had become accustomed.

In my most gentlemanly fashion, I told her she was crazy. To be sure, she would receive income from those bonds, but that income would be fixed for a long period of time, say, twenty years. During that long stretch, inflation would eat up her fixed income so it would mean less and less to her, year by year. Consider mixing some bonds with some long-term growth stocks, I suggested. You don't want to sacrifice all chances for growth. You don't want to sacrifice all hedges against inflation.

She bought none of it. She knew what she wanted, and that included a portfolio that would not build anything to be left to her two stepchildren, whom she hated.

At her insistence, and that of her lawyers, we decided to comply. Bought the foolish woman a million bucks worth of bonds.

In six months, she was complaining. "John, you've got to come out to see me," she said, and I went for tea. Well, she had heard all about this stock and that stock at a party, and they were growing so fast, and also paying high dividends. "Why don't you put me into nice stocks like those?" she demanded to know.

"But if you recall," I told her softly, "when we set up your portfolio, that was not what you wanted at all. You were quite insistent on bonds, Mrs. Jameson, bonds. And we did what you wanted."

She said nothing, but glowered at me.

"Do you want us to change now; is that what you're saying? We can do it. But I must caution you that if we were to do that, say, sell half your bonds and reinvest it in stocks, you'd suffer a big loss on those bonds, and you would end up with much less current income."

She sighed. "What I don't understand is why we didn't do something like this in the beginning, six months ago? Why didn't we put a third of my money into stocks?"

"Mrs. Jameson, in all fairness, I'm sure you remember that I was urging you to consider precisely some arrangement along those lines. But I couldn't convince you of it."

"Oh, you should have known better. Couldn't you tell I was so upset by the death of my husband that I didn't really make sense at that time? You should have simply gone ahead and done it..."

By the end of the first year, she was ready to sue us, but she satisfied herself by moving her trust to some other bank, where presumably people could read her mind better than we could. Mrs. Jameson was not atypical.

After nine years in trusts, I began to get restless. I had moved up rapidly, but now I could see that progress was blocked. Both my boss and the man over him were not that much older than I. And though I had learned an awful lot in trusts, and I enjoyed much of the job of trust officer, I began to wonder how long I should stay where I was and what my next step might be. I got some clear answers one day in one of those monthly Investment Committee review meetings.

Those were very serious affairs. All of us in the big conference room; each of your accounts flashed onto a huge screen; your boss, his boss, two members of the Board of Trustees of the bank examining every move you've made with each client's money.

Careers were made and broken in those sessions. If you couldn't answer the questions, or you answered, but it was clear you simply were not on top of your accounts, that was conveyed in various quiet ways to the president of the bank, to the other board members, and your career was finished at The Bank of New York. You wouldn't be fired, but you wouldn't be given another good job in the entire organization, no matter how long you stayed around.

When I was an assistant trust officer and had to make presentations, I'd spend five days doing nothing else but preparing, always up till two A.M. the night before.

But as a group head, I had my assistants make the presentation and stay up till two in the morning. I'd rehearse them, but all I had to do was sit in on the meeting, once or twice interject an answer, and generally look and sound omniscient.

Then one Wednesday, one of my assistants called in with the flu. He couldn't present his accounts that day, and worse, I had not even rehearsed him, so I had no real familiarity with them. All I could do was take his

sixty-plus accounts into the meeting, explain to everyone what had happened, and tell them I would try to
review and defend them as best I could.

I was brilliant. As I flashed one after another on the
screen I recalled how we had set them up two years
before, three years before, how I had convinced the
young heiress to put this portion into blue chips and that
portion into growth stocks, and on and on. I fielded
every question flawlessly.

The whole performance was so good that after the
meeting my boss, only half in jest, said: "You set us up,
didn't you?"

And that night, thinking it all through, I knew I had
to move on. It was all getting too easy. I had to get out
and start something new.

Commercial banking and the real action

Somehow, my restlessness began to show, even though
I wasn't aware of it. But my boss picked up the signals,
and before I had more than two undercover meetings
with headhunters, my boss came to me with a most
unusual offer. Would I consider leaving trusts and going
over to the commercial side? Our big branch at Fifth
Avenue needed a group head.

What was so special about this was that in our bank
as all others, trusts and commercial are worlds apart.
Commercial includes all the retail business, all the
checking and savings accounts, all the consumer and
business loans that most people use a bank for. Commercial are the people in their dark suits whom you see
looking down at their desks when you go into your
bank.

Commercial traditionally looks down on trusts. They
say trusts account for only about 5 percent of the
earnings of the bank, yet it's got all that staff. They're
not real bankers, goes the charge, they're just there to
keep the Mrs. Jamesons happy.

In a sense, the charge is accurate. Trust departments were set up to accommodate rich folk and to insure that they won't feel they have to take their banking elsewhere. In fact, most trust departments lose money, and a number of banks have tried to get out of that business, but once you are named a trustee, it is practically impossible to untangle yourself from the legal responsibilities.

So, it is rare indeed to move from a good spot in trusts to one in commercial, and when I reported the first day to Fifth Avenue, there was quite a bit of muffled fanfare.

Obviously, by this point I had a strong investment background, and I had shown certain managerial talents. I was also a good salesman, with some notable success at bringing new business into the bank. All of that was needed for the new job.

What I didn't have was any idea of how to make a loan. So, to learn that and familiarize myself in general with this side of the bank, I went through a new twelve-week training program.

It was an interesting program, but I never learned from it how to make a good loan. That, as I would see, would only come after I had been trying to do it for months and months. And though it might seem odd, this is the way personal loan officers are still trained, or not trained. The real learning comes on the job.

I started with four to five weeks in the Corporate Credit Department, where we took apart companies and analyzed their financial health. These were all companies doing business with us, and we had to figure out if our money was still safe with them and whether we should think about lending them more. So I learned about current ratios, what the book value of their stock was compared with its market price, and how they handled their debt. I learned how to "spread those numbers," how to extract all the important data from a corporation's own report and fit it into our own categories.

Though corporate lending is more complex than personal lending, and the numbers are almost always bigger, it is a pretty mechanical process, and so to me, simpler. What matters most with those loans are the numbers. What's the cash flow? What are the accounts receivable? The liabilities? Their projections, our projections? Their ability to repay? It's all computed by formulas.

The people who manage a company affect your thinking, but your decision is primarily based on those numbers. Numbers are important in personal lending too. But there, I learned, decisions are infinitely more subjective.

I could begin to see the difference when I got into the department called Miscellaneous Reviews. People in this department spend their time reevaluating all loans that are not simple installment loans that the bank has made to individuals and small businesses. Over and over again, I saw them question, first, the real purpose of the loan. Did it make sense for that particular businessman? Then, they focused on the ability to pay back. How did the lending officer expect the business-man to pay us back? How closely had the officer exam-ined the man's earnings? His assets, his possibilities for future earnings? Were all the payments being made on time? How was the payment schedule agreed upon, anyway?

Those were the questions the miscellaneous review people asked themselves and, once every eighteen months, asked of the officer who had made the actual loans. If there was any doubt about the soundness of a loan, it had to be defended by the officer who had made it, and those were not friendly meetings.

I began to realize what it meant to lend money and expect to be paid back. I began to realize that a human being will say one thing, and really mean it, but still not be able to deliver on that commitment.

I began to see that as a loan officer I would have to figure out for myself what that human being was actual-ly capable of doing, good intentions and promises aside, and then attach some probabilities to it.

I learned that, to a degree, the bank had already done that. It knew that something like 1.8 percent of all loans made would not be paid back, and the cost of those loans was already written into the other 98.2 percent. So in a sense, the bank didn't have to worry all that much. They were covering their bets. It was you who would have to cope with the dunning and the lawyers.

One day I had a brilliant insight. "Supposing we set up a loan for a year," I asked one of the officers I was working under, "and we let it slide for two years. What difference does it make? We collect all that extra interest, don't we?"

"You're not being paid just to collect interest," he said. "If you set up a payment plan on a loan and your customer doesn't pay according to the plan, then everything is endangered. The whole point is to collect the interest *and* get your money back, so you can lend it out to someone else. That's what makes it a business."

Tellers are special creatures

Some of the departments I moved through were plain boring, but then much of the work done in any bank is boring. Check processing, for example, where I sat for a week, numbed as I watched clerks sort out all the checks the bank paid each day and file them into the folders of individual accounts.

I spent a few days with the tellers, one of them behind the cage, and that was fairly interesting because it was a busy day. Tellers are trained to ignore the frowns and sighs and shifting of feet of customers in those lines. But it's an impossible thing to do, and I could see why. That impatience palpably enshrouds the place. They are also trained to be most careful when things are the busiest. That is when most errors are made and when professionals try their little schemes, taking advantage of the lines, the pressure to speed things up and rip off $25, $50 from a harried teller.

They are a special breed, tellers, and good ones are

not easy to find. The job doesn't pay well; for the most part it's fairly dull, even though in its way, important. About 85 percent of all the people doing business in a bank never have any contact with anyone but tellers.

Banks are always looking for good tellers. Not always in the market for trust officers, or investment analysts, but always after good tellers.

Usually they are high school graduates, possibly with a bit of college, or putting themselves through college.

The bank is looking, first, for someone who will absolutely follow orders and procedures. Stop doing that now and do this because that's the procedure, no matter how big the lines are, how the customers are grumbling.

Tellers are trained not to make any judgments. Yes, he looks honest, but don't you decide. Get an officer from the platform to decide if we should cash that check.

The second thing the bank looks for in a teller is someone who doesn't want to or need to steal money from them. So, if there is a young woman who has recently graduated from high school, and she's living at home, has her basic expenses covered, but needs some money for clothes, for evenings out with friends, she fits nicely. Or, as with many of the older female tellers, they are supplementing their husbands' incomes. Or, the person who is going to college at night and needs the money to help pay tuition. But not someone who has to pay a mortgage off on his or her teller's salary.

Tellers rarely move up. They are hired for that one job, and they stay there. The turnover is high. Being a teller for a few years suggests a certain dependability and honesty about a young person, useful in moving on to better paying jobs.

Handling all that cash, they obviously have opportunities to steal, and a certain number do. Because banks are so careful, it's fairly limited.

We had one teller who specialized in little old ladies,

particularly those with failing sight. One would come in and deposit, say, $280 in her savings account, and he'd enter it in her savings book as $260. Then, a bit later in the day, he'd pocket that $20.

He was also good at taking advantage of the confusion from multiple transactions; someone would come to him with, for example, a savings deposit, a mixed cash and check deposit for a checking account, and a check to be cashed. A pleasant young man with a trusting smile, he could slip another $20 out of that pile of papers.

I had a friend at another bank who worked as a teller while going through college, and he told me that he regularly pocketed $40 to $50 on Mondays and Fridays, the two busiest days in his bank. "Lines are long, people in a hurry to get back to work. A guy cashes a check for $188.90. I give him $178.90, lots of fives, tens, singles. He's half an hour late to get back to the office, probably won't even count it. And if he does, I count it all over again, very slowly, apologize, mutter about the lines—'get so rushed you don't know what you're doin'—and smile."

There are cameras scanning tellers' cages, but they are meant for armed robbers, not tellers. They have their backs to the cameras anyway. It is quite simple to palm a couple of tens and slip them into your pocket.

Every bank maintains an elaborate internal security department. But security wouldn't start watching a particular teller unless they got awfully suspicious.

Watching out for mistakes

The best thing to do, if you're making a multiple transaction and you expect to get cash back, is to figure it all out ahead of time and write the cash due you on a slip of paper. Even honest tellers make mistakes processing complicated transactions.

Also, if you are making a cash deposit, be sure that the teller puts a pencil mark under the figure you have entered as "cash," at the top of the deposit slip. That's an important signal, alerting the terminal operator who will be punching your deposit into the computer at the end of the day that you have in fact made that "cash" deposit, and it is to be credited to your account immediately, as opposed to a "checks" deposit, which will require clearance time before you get credit.

By the way, if a teller makes a mistake, gives you $10 more than he or she is supposed to, the money does not come out of his meager pay. At the end of each banking day, each teller has to add and subtract and prove out all the transactions of the day with the cash he started out with in his own "bank," as the cash drawer is called. If it doesn't prove out, he'll be kept there by the head teller until the error can be spotted. But even then, if a teller is short, he doesn't have to make it up himself. However, if a teller comes up short or long on a regular basis, and it doesn't matter which, that teller will be looking for another job. Which is one reason why a teller will get even more deliberate and careful in direct response to the pressure of longer lines.

It is not the tellers who are responsible for those long lines everyone suffers, even though they usually take the spoken and unspoken blame for them. Those lines are there because every bank has done the same studies, and applied what is known as the Queueing Theory, and come up with the same conclusion: It is too expensive to have extra tellers just for rush periods.

Most of the day, most days, tellers have very little to do. Then the crush comes, the worst in every bank in America hitting on Friday afternoon, when everyone is depositing or cashing pay checks.

Nobody has figured out an efficient and economic way to supplement the regular underused tellers during those short stretches when the demand is highest. So, all banks do the same thing: let you stand, wait, and suffer. Hardly anyone, experience has shown them, pulls his account out of a bank due to lines. Because everyone knows that conditions are not going to be any better at the bank down the block.

It is the head tellers who have the real opportunities to steal. The biggest case I ever heard of was about five years ago, when the head teller of one of New York's leading savings banks lifted $1.2 million.

Having access to all the accounts, he selected large savings accounts that had not had any interest posted in them for long periods of time. The interest was accumulating, but it wasn't being posted in the passbooks because the depositors, again mostly little old ladies, didn't have any need to bother with those accounts. The money was there, they knew, safe, they assumed, interest accumulating, and that was the way the world was supposed to be.

He borrowed from those sleepy accounts and went to the track. When he was finally caught, he had blown $1.2 million, and not a word hit the newspapers. I learned of it from a senior officer in our bank, who said something about too close for comfort. Their main branch was a few blocks from us.

In the great tradition of our business, the savings bank covered every penny their head teller had stolen and quietly dismissed the fellow. Couldn't prosecute and have the whole scandal in the papers scaring away all those trusting little old ladies.

The startling effect you have on bankers

One of the most important lessons for my new job in personal banking, I absorbed rather than learned. It is the way bankers on the floor perceive you, the public. They don't trust you. In fact, they fear you.

That might come as something of a surprise, since I'm sure that you go into your bank and approach any bank officer with great trepidation and fear of rejection.

But let me tell you, he sits there feeling anxious and vulnerable.

To begin with, he absorbs some of the attitude from the auditing department of his bank. Their basic point of view is that customers, given half a chance, will lie, cheat, and steal. Of course, auditors spend all their time investigating fraud, theft, and anything that looks at all suspicious, so it's not surprising that their perception is somewhat warped.

Still, the loan officer at his desk is aware of certain facts. To start with, he knows there is this mass of people out there, and he doesn't know any of them. All strangers, and you don't like to lend money to strangers.

Further, he has been informed of some statistics. He knows that a meaningful percentage of that mass of strangers are crooks, that another meaningful percentage might intend to be honest, but even so, they will not be able to pay back any money he lends them. Beyond that, he has the experience of being there. In truth, when you're on the floor, you never know what's going to come at you. You even begin to feel physically vulnerable.

So the senior officers take the desks that are farthest away from the railing. They not only put distance and troops between you and them, but they literally protect their flanks. Nobody can sneak up on their side, or their back, unseen.

The meaning and impact of all this hit me on my first tumultuous day on the floor.

Though I'd had considerable responsibility as a trust officer, supervising some 600 accounts, about $420 million in investments, everything was removed and quiet. Everything was under control.

On the floor of the Fifth Avenue branch, my whole neat, controlled world cracked. Suddenly, I was in one way or another responsible for 3,000 accounts, people I didn't know, who were out there writing checks, overdrawing, possibly stealing the bank's money. Mrs. Jameson could be difficult and self-destructive, but at least she did it over tea.

Now, I began to develop a completely different attitude toward customers. I was no longer a confidant, listening with real or feigned sympathy to real or imagined concerns. With these strangers, it was us against them.

I discovered a whole new set of worries. If I made a mistake in judgment and landed a $10,000 loan for someone who didn't pay it back, officially the bank wrote it off. To some degree, they had even anticipated it as a cost of doing business. But unofficially, I learned, that mistake was held against me. It could mean no raise in pay for a while, no promotion.

Obviously, worries of this sort can make a bank officer absolutely paranoid and rigid. I could see it happening to me. I'd finish talking with one customer, who, in fact, was not to be trusted, and I'd carry my suspicions right over to the next person who sat down at my desk.

After working on it, I think I was able to control that occupational paranoia, but an awful lot of bank officers never do. They are among the worst you meet. They start with their suspicions and layer on a few generalizations, creating instant portraits: You've been working in the same job less than a year, recently divorced, no longer own your own home—that's all they have to hear. They know everything about you, they decide, and you're a bad risk. The facts, of course, might be quite different. You might be starting life over and be the best loan risk you have ever been. But such frightened people are unable to suspend their pervasive fears to see and deal with individuals.

The shock of the first day on the floor is dramatic for everyone. Mine became a kind of special total immersion because of a bit of bureaucratic confusion. The officer who was vacating my intended desk wasn't ready to leave, when I arrived. He had three days to go, before he went downtown. So, instead of being able to settle in, hunker down there, back in the relative security of the middle rows, I was assigned a temporary desk right up front. Not only right up front, but the

first desk you saw as you came into the bank. It was like
being "point" on a jungle patrol. I survived there a day
and a half.

Anybody with a question on his mind, a problem to
settle, came through the front door and marched directly to my desk. "I need a car loan..." "My statement
has an error this month..." "I'm going to sue you
people if you bounce one more check on me..."

Some people had reasonable business, but I couldn't
do anything for them, or do any of my other work
either, because I had become a complaint bureau.
People came in, sat down at my desk, and wouldn't
leave. I needed an air traffic controller.

After the first day, I went to the head of the branch
and asked him if he could move me somewhere,
anywhere, to a vault if necessary, until my desk was
ready. He patted me on the shoulder, told me to hang
in there, probably only another day at most.

I didn't make it through another day. Between eleven
the next morning and noon, a guy on a unicycle rode up
to my desk, wanting a loan for $25,000, "fast, man,"
after which Mr. Sommerville had his little accident.

An elderly, distinguished-looking gray-haired man, an
old client of the bank, Mr. Sommerville paused at my
desk for some reason, and while stating his business,
lost control of his bowels. Incontinence it is called, and
it affects rich and poor alike at a certain age.

I spent the next half hour assisting Mr. Sommerville
through his ritual in the men's room, after ordering the
guard to clean up the mess in front of my desk. And
then spent another half hour trying to locate Mr.
Sommerville's daughter. It took her about half an hour
to come down to the bank to collect her father, who
passed that time sitting at my desk, babbling to me
about what was wrong with America.

In fact, having a desk in such a vulnerable position
can be dangerous for the bank as well as its employees.
We had a case of a con man who took advantage of a
busy lunchtime period to confuse a young woman who

was working there. Something about his taxi waiting outside, and he'd miss his plane if she didn't cash his travelers checks immediately. And so she did, even though he didn't have an account with our branch, and she couldn't verify the man or his signature. The fellow earned himself $3,500 on stolen travelers checks. After that one, the desk was moved.

Chapter 4

How to deal
with a frightened
banker: Take
him to lunch

When you think about it, the truth here is amusing. Up to now, I suspect, you always thought of the man in the gray suit as solid confidence.

But in fact, his fears are just as real as yours, if different. He doesn't have to worry about being rejected by you, but he's got all those other concerns nonetheless.

Add to that the nature of the beast. As we have seen, banks attract people to work there who want order, who are by nature careful, cautious, who are paid to be conservative in their judgment and their demeanor.

At the same time, these same dry people are paid to do business with the uncontrollable masses who are continually swirling about them. They must not only confront this mob, they must extract business from it, and good business at that.

It is the irony of this situation that offers you a great opportunity. You must cope with your banker's fears. If you do, you will get service from your bank that you never imagined possible.

To start with, you must separate yourself from that faceless mob. When you do that, you eliminate your banker's mob phobia, and you also create two extremely important new conditions. First, you will get your banker's attention. And second, you will personalize your relationship with him. Only when you have done that will your banker really start to work for you.

The dreaded "walk-in"

Never, never start a relationship with a bank by "walking in" and going to the nearest bank officer and announcing, "I want to open an account."

Do that, and you are, in his mind, a "walk-in," and you lose. You are interrupting his work, and worse, coming at him unexpectedly. Beyond that, you are not being what he considers "businesslike." If he can spin you off down into the vulgar pits of the Special Checking Accounts, he will.

Begin your approach to a new bank by doing something few people ever do: Find out something about the bank, before you go in there. You should know what you're getting into and not pop into a bank just because it's a block from your office.

Perhaps just as importantly, any information you can learn about a bank can be used to impress and influence the prospective bank officer when you finally do sit down at his desk to open your account.

So, call a friend or relative who uses the bank you're considering, or who uses any bank other than your own, if you intend to change and aren't yet sure where to go. It should be someone who is roughly in your financial category, requiring more or less what you do from a bank. Ask them about the service they get and the problems they have with their bank. What is their bank especially good at? How satisfied are they?

If you work for a company, talk with someone in your

company's treasurer's office. Who is the company's bank? Your treasurer's office is important to the company's bank.

One of the very best ways to start a relationship with a bank is to go to it recommended by, or at the suggestion of, your company's treasurer, assistant treasurer, anyone from your company who has some business relationship with the bank.

Whether the lead comes from a friend, relative, or company officer, it is terribly important that you get the name of a specific bank officer to contact. Whom do they do business with? That's who you want. Remember, the whole strategy here is to remove yourself from those blurred unruly masses and personalize your relationship.

Once you have the bank officer's name, call him or her, even if that person is obviously wrong for you. If the treasurer of your company puts you on to the head of corporate banking, you know he is not the officer for your checking account. Doesn't matter, make that first call to him anyway, and let him tell you that, as much as he'd like to help you himself, he handles only corporate affairs these days, but the person you should talk with is Mrs. DeGraff, and what he'd like to do is tell Mrs. DeGraff that you'd like to talk with her, and she'll be getting a call from you. And you can be sure he will tell Mrs. DeGraff. He'll also tell her how important your company and your treasurer are to the bank. I assure you, Mrs. DeGraff will be so happy to hear from you, you might just weep.

Using your company's bank is one of the best things you can do for yourself. You multiply your clout by that of the whole company.

You will also get a warm reception, if your attorney, accountant, or investment adviser sends you to his banker.

Banks are partial to those people. Not only do they tend to earn good money themselves, and keep nice balances in their accounts, but they are all in occupations where they can send lots of clients to their own banks. It's another way you can use someone else's clout to your own advantage.

If you start out with any of those introductions, you will get the banker's attention. Now you have to keep it.

Getting "businesslike"

First make an appointment with him or her.

I cannot overemphasize how important this simple step is. After all, you wouldn't pop into your lawyer's office or your accountant's office without an appointment. Treat your bank officer the same way.

In fact, make the appointment at the bank officer's convenience. That tells him a few wonderful things about you.

It tells him that you're "businesslike," and as you can imagine, he loves that. "Businesslike" to him translates into someone who is probably able to handle his financial affairs, someone who takes banking and, therefore, his money seriously. Someone who won't give him extraordinary problems. Someone who won't waste his time.

No matter how well recommended you come, if you don't make an appointment but walk in off the street, you are still stigmatized as a "walk-in" and it'll take a lot to erase that terrible epithet from his mind.

If you have some real business to bring to the bank, more than a modest checking account, perhaps a personal checking account with four-figure balances, a spouse's account to follow, and an account for your own business, I'd do more than make an appointment. I'd take a banker to lunch.

After all, you are considering a real business relationship, almost a partnership with that new bank. You better make sure they will give you the attention and services you're going to require. It can be critical to your business. You'd better be sure that the man or woman whom you're going to have on the other end of the phone every week or so is more than simply pleasant. You want to be sure that person has some grasp of your business, so he or she can respond intelligently when you need him.

You also want the banker to perceive you in the right light, from the very beginning. If you can call and tell him that his bank has been recommended by your friend, Mr. Treasurer at Valued Client, Inc., and you're interested in moving your banking business, he's immediately attentive. If you then ask him if he might have a lunch free in the next week or so, he knows how serious you are. "If you have the time, I'd certainly appreciate it. Give us both a good chance to consider what I'm looking for, and whether my business would make sense to you people . . ." He's all ears and eyes.

Next, a very simple piece of advice: Dress appropriately. When it comes to first impressions, bankers are like everyone else. Given what I've told you about them, you can easily imagine how they respond to you if you come in wearing blue jeans instead of what they consider "business clothes."

Dressing appropriately also means dressing the way you normally do in your work. Walk in wearing a blue pinstripe suit, white shirt, and dark tie for a first meeting with a bank officer at the City National Bank in Beverly Hills, and you're in trouble.

What to say and not say

An early warning note for the first encounter with your prospective new banker:

Do not try to impress him with numbers.

In the first place, you probably don't have amounts

that are going to impress him anyway. Beyond that, numbers come later. What you want to do at this stage of things is establish a good feeling in him. In a way, you want to sell yourself to him, in such a way that he will very definitely want to sell himself and his bank to you.

Start out by giving him reasons, the right reasons for leaving your present bank.

Be careful here. Don't launch an angry mega-attack full of generalized complaints on Old Faithful Trust Company. If you do, he might quickly label you a "bouncer." A "bouncer" is what we call a person who bounces from one bank to another, never satisfied with anything. A "bouncer" is to be avoided, as quickly as possible. If he sniffs you as one, he doesn't want to bother with your business because he knows you're going to be nothing but headaches for him, and no matter what he does, how much time he gives to your problems, he's going to be your next victim. In fact, in self-defense, he's going to have to keep a special file on you to have all the evidence he needs when you leave, and his boss wants to know why. He knows that in a year or so, you'll be having another meeting just like this one with another banker moaning about the abuse you suffered from him.

At the same time, obviously, he expects you to have some complaints about your present bank. If you weren't dissatisfied, why would you want to change?

"I've been doing business with them for three years," you tell him, "and I've simply had enough. I'm a reasonably patient person, and I know we all make mistakes, but I can't get basic banking services from them. It's little things and big things. I can't get my statements from them on time, a little thing, but an annoyance. Whenever I have a short-term transaction with them—like a Certificate of Deposit—I need a few days notification when the CD is coming due, so I can decide whether to turn it over or take the money out. Twenty-four hours before it's due, I get a phone call. Never fails. No matter how often I tell them that's not enough time. And on top of everything else, they're rude . . . Yes, I mean it. You look surprised, but believe me, they are just plain rude."

If he hears complaints along those lines, he is not only relieved, he is delighted to have a shot at the account. You have given Old Faithful a fair chance; their service has been lousy, and they have not improved it. Worst of all, they have been rude. To him, that is unforgivable. That not only violates the gentlemanly and ladylike code of behavior, it's stupid.

Rudeness only infuriates a customer and, quite possibly, brings your boss down on your head. If the customer is angry enough, he'll write a letter to the president of the bank. The president does not like to hear that his officers are rude, nor does he want to be bothered with such a problem. He's running a bank, not a prep school. He doesn't want to waste his time reprimanding you, but he's got to do something. He calls your boss and takes the time to explain. All an unnecessary waste of everyone's time, and it still might result in a lost account. Now your prospective banker is warming to you as a new account. Coddle him further with something along these lines: "So, I'm afraid I've had all I can take from those people. Your bank, on the other hand, has been highly recommended to me by my good friend (or colleague at Valued Client, Inc.), and so I thought it would be good if we could have a talk to see if you'd like my account . . . see if we can work together . . . if my account makes sense to you people . . ."

To a banker, there is a huge difference between that and someone who says, "I want to open an account."

You might add something more: "By the way, in addition to my friend Henry's recommendation, I'm also impressed with the general reputation your bank has . . ."

If he hears words like those, he very much wants your account, and the conversation slides into specifics, the kind of account or accounts you need. And the amount you're prepared to deposit.

Obviously, on one level, the amount matters to him.

It is hardly the only thing he's interested in, but if you are able to open with, say, $2,000 in your personal Regular Checking Account, so much the better. If you can put together $5,000 for starters, all his instincts about you are confirmed.

But don't despair. Even if you can start with only $200, or $500, he remains interested in you because of the way you approached him and talked to him.

Besides, what is perhaps just as important to him as the initial deposit you make is your potential.

Anybody who approaches him in the businesslike manner you showed is, in his mind, going to do well. That's the way he'll see you. You might be in the lower reaches of your company today, but you will be rising.

Also, he can see in you the possibility of more than one account. Maybe he can get you to do all your banking with him—your personal accounts, your savings accounts, those of your husband or wife. That's a form of potential and it matters.

In fact, most people are much better off putting all their major accounts in one bank, especially if they do it at the beginning of their dealings with the bank. It gives you that much more clout and leverage. If you spread yourself out over two or three banks, you won't mean much to any of them.

What he should offer you

Once the signature cards and other details are taken care of, sit back and listen to your new banker. Let him perform an aria or two about how wonderful his bank is and about all the glittering special services they're going to offer you.

If he doesn't launch into this, beware. Perhaps he's really not impressed with you and your business. Or, perhaps, he doesn't have the clout you thought he had. You might have to go over his head, actually get your accounts transferred to another officer. Or, perhaps he doesn't have much interest in his own job. Always possible.

But he should be saying to you something like: "I hope you can get to know our bank over a period of time. I think we have about the best investment management team in town. And I know we have the best people there are when it comes to trusts and estate planning. Even if some of this might be a bit premature for your situation at the moment, it seems to me these are some areas you should be giving thought to a little down the road, and I shouldn't think too far down the road. Of course, anything you need in the way of a personal or business loan . . . that's what we're here for."

When you hear the magic word "loan," try to control yourself, especially when he makes it sound as if he wants to give you a few thousand bucks right there and then as a little gift, a token of his sincerity and thanks, to make you feel really loved and wanted in your new bank home.

Don't scare the dear banker, by jerking forward at "loan." He might think you weren't very sincere after all, and all you want is a loan from him because you haven't been able to qualify for one at your previous bank.

Keep the conversation on the services. "Yes, indeed, I have begun to think quite a bit about estate planning," you might say. "And in fact, one of the things that attracted me to you people in the first place was your terrific reputation in that area."

Or: "To be honest with you, the amount of investing I do isn't nearly enough, I'm sure, to be of interest to you people. But I see it growing all the time, and at some point, I would very much welcome a conversation with your investment people . . ."

Don't feel you have to tell and show him everything at this session. After all, it is only your first date. Bankers know that people normally don't like to reveal themselves and their financial worth right off. Only natural, and if you do otherwise, a good banker will be wary.

Still, if you maintain some nice assets—a fairly substantial portfolio at Shearson Loeb Rhodes, for example—
let him know. Only increases your appeal. Makes you
seem ever more valuable and alluring, and starts him
wondering, "What do I have to do . . . what kind of
special treatment do I have to give, before we can get
that portfolio moved over here for us to manage . . ."

You will leave the bank feeling good. You will feel
wanted. You will feel, probably for the first time in your
life, that you now have a relationship with a bank in
which a bank officer actually knows who you are and
cares about you.

When he calls in a couple of weeks, pretending that
he simply wanted to be sure you received all your checks
for your various accounts, to be sure that everything is
okay, and wonders if you might be free for lunch soon,
say next Wednesday, and perhaps you'd like to come
into the bank—"We have a pleasant private dining
room here, food isn't three stars perhaps, but not bad.
And it is quiet. Give us a chance to talk a bit."—When
that call comes, you know you are well on your way.
You most definitely have his attention.

Checklist:

Starting with a new bank

1. Gather intelligence on various banks. Don't go to the nearest one simply because it's there.
2. At all costs, avoid becoming a "walk-in." Get the name of a bank officer to contact.
3. If possible, use the clout of a friend or your company.
4. Call for a "businesslike" appointment.
5. Avoid mega-blasts on your old bank. Do not sound like a "bouncer."
6. Intrigue the bank officer with your "potential" as a customer.
7. Steer the conversation to all those juicy "Special Services."

Chapter 5

Getting service out of your old bank, at last

Maybe you don't want or need a new bank, but you are still bothered by the feeling that you have absolutely no personal contact with anyone in your bank, and even though they're holding just about every penny you own, they don't know you from a number.

Your feeling of anonymity is well founded. In fact, unless you change things, you *are* nothing but an account number to them.

First, you've got to find the right bank officer to connect with.

Chances are, up to now, no matter how long you've had your account there, you've never dealt with only one person in the bank, your person. If you had a problem that went beyond the cheerful Mrs. Sullivan, your regular teller, you asked the bank guard whom you should talk to, and he shunted you to the nearest open desk.

Those days of second-class citizenship are over. Call your bank and ask to speak to the bank officer who handles your account. As simple as that. Every bank has some kind of system for calls like this. Either the operator directs you to the officer, after a question or two, an answer or two from you, or she puts you onto someone with a directory.

When you've been transferred to Mrs. Allen, you'll be a bit surprised because you've seen Mrs. Allen sitting at her desk, noted her nameplate on the corner of her desk a hundred times, but never connected her with yourself.

All that will now change. You and Mrs. Allen are about to mean something to each other. The reason for this call is for you to set up an appointment with Mrs. Allen.

If you're wondering what excuse you give to Mrs. Allen for this appointment, it's as complicated as saying, "Mrs. Allen, I have a few questions about my account, and I wonder if you have a few minutes in the course of the next week when I might come in and review things with you?"

If you're wondering and worrying about what you are actually going to say to Mrs. Allen when your summit meeting comes, relax. Obviously, your situation is different from the person who is going to Mrs. Allen to open a new account. So your line of discussion will be different too.

When you see Mrs. Allen, you are in fact going to review your account and, for the first time, inform her of your generally bright financial condition in the world. And, as we'll see, you are going to open the door to the land of Special Services, and establish yourself as a Preferred Customer.

If you work for a fair-sized company, you might want to use the company's leverage at the bank, instead of calling Mrs. Allen directly. You might go the route I spoke of earlier, have a corporate financial officer make the call to the corporate lending officer he deals with. That officer in turn will bounce you over to Mrs. Allen.

Either way, between the phone call and the time you sit down at Mrs. Allen's desk, she'll have pulled out

your file and reviewed it. She may find the facts of your
banking life are not all that appealing. Average balance:
$300. One car loan, paid off over thirty-six months.
Records show no particular trouble with the customer,
but not that much money, either. I wonder what he
wants?

Do not be dismayed. Even though your banking
biography does not excite Mrs. Allen, she will hardly
dismiss you.

Simply the fact that you called for an appointment, or
had a corporate friend make a call, alerts her. Remember,
by those gestures, you are, in her mind, "businesslike."
There are all sorts of good reasons, she can imagine,
why you might want to see her. She knows that people
get big raises and promotions, for example, or inherit
money. She knows that customers can be transformed
from ugly ducklings to prince charmings overnight. She
is up on her Cinderella stories. After all, how long does
it take for someone to learn of a new job? How long
does it take for a will to be read?

Mrs. Allen, I assure you, will give you all her attention when you appear for your appointment. Now, to
keep that attention.

Making life brighter for Mrs. Allen and yourself

The way, essentially, is to play on Mrs. Allen's fondest
dreams, without getting too carried away by the game.

Mrs. Allen's dream for you couldn't be nicer. She
wants you to become successful and rich. And then,
you will bring her more business and greater happiness.

So, give her hope. Let her know in your first meeting
that since you opened your account two or three years
ago, there have been a number of happy developments
in your financial life. You don't want to lie to Mrs.
Allen, because she has a very good nose for lies. But
you can suggest or allude to various promotions that

you have already received, as well as to others that your boss assures you are soon to come.

Maybe, in truth, you have a parent or a relative of some means who is aging. Not to be ghoulish, but the death of that person might well change your entire financial profile, and that's something you should be thinking about anyway.

With such an inheritance or not, what you and Mrs. Allen are both gazing at is the future, the brighter the better.

I find that most people never think of their financial futures. Businesses do, but not people. Businesses, even small ones, are continually looking ahead, spinning out projections and saying, well, six months from now, we should be here, and two years from now, if things go the way they should, we ought to be over here. But people go from paycheck to paycheck.

Try to think of yourself as a small business. As soon as you do, you'll realize that like any small business, you've got possibilities for growth. And like any small business, you need to do some basic planning.

That's essentially what you should convey to Mrs. Allen. You are looking ahead. Right now, the way you see things, you're at a take-off stage of economic development. In fact, if it suits your fantasies and style better, think of yourself as a modestly small underdeveloped country, where there's every reason to believe oil lies under your surface. New surveys indicate it could be a big field. As the Minister of Finance for your own relatively small underdeveloped nation, you have the responsibility to do some planning on the exciting possibility that there might soon be a huge strike. Black gold all over the place, and you want to be prepared.

(Not to get too carried away with this notion, but to a degree, it's a healthy metaphor to bear in mind, thinking of yourself as a steamy, tiny underdeveloped nation. Banks understand those places very well. In fact, American banks presently have billions of dollars in outstanding debts to such exotic customers. That's *billions*.

They're called LDC loans for Less Developed Countries. The likelihood of those less developed chaps ever paying back those loans is so slight that the banks have no real choice except to keep lending them more money or rolling over the existing loans. A billion comes due, a finance minister sweeps into the bank's executive suite swirling his brightly colored robes, slyly shaking his gold chains, smiling very broadly. A summit conference, and the finance minister steps back out to his limousine, smiling even more broadly. The bank has just agreed to extend the loan for five years, at the same rate of interest, and he has agreed to at least try and pay off the interest, more or less on time. Paying off the billions of principal owed is not even seriously discussed. When things reach such a stage, instead of a bank-customer relationship, there is a bank-customer partnership. In a partnership, as opposed to a relationship, your problems are the bank's problems. A much more comfortable arrangement if you're a steamy, tiny under-developed nation.)

As I said, do not get too carried away. Do not come sweeping in yourself in some rented tribal toga. Mrs. Allen might not have a great sense of humor.

Rather, dressed in your normal business clothes, tell Mrs. Allen about the brightness of your future. Tell her that as part of your planning, you would like to avail yourself of a few of the bank's services, which you've only heard vaguely about.

You want to steer the discussion into the area of Special Services. Overdraft checking plans, investment advice, estate planning, special credit plans, all the services that copy the real services your bank gives automatically to rich folk, the true Preferred Customers or, as they are sometimes called, High Net Worth Individuals.

In Chapter 13, we'll take a close look at the precious world inhabited by bankers and their rich customers. Most people have no idea what their bank does for richies. Once you have a picture of it, you will have a dream model of what to go after for yourself.

You should get Mrs. Allen to enlighten you, and all you have to do is start the discussion in that direction.

"Just how does this Convenience Credit Plan work, Mrs. Allen?"

She'll be only too happy to tell you.

Taking services, even if you don't need them

A strategy point: At this stage of things, you are not so much interested in the services as you are in establishing a relationship with Mrs. Allen.

You might, for example, sign up for Convenience Credit, or whatever your bank calls overdraft checking. You might not need it at the moment, but you don't have to pay for it until you use it. The point is, you're doing some business with Mrs. Allen. The same goes for any credit card system your bank might be selling.

If estate planning in its full regal form is pointless for you right now, there are certainly some aspects of your financial life that do need planning. Insurance? Will?

Ask her about such matters. Even if you decide to wait, you have informed her, signaled her that you are serious, that you are planning.

You might not be able to think about an investment portfolio without giggling. Try not to, and tell her instead that such investing is premature for you at the moment, but before long you expect things might change, and you wonder whom you should talk to when that day arrives. You give Mrs. Allen ever more hope, and she should respond: "Just give me a call, and I'll put you with our investment people. I think they're tops."

"So I've heard, Mrs. Allen, so I've heard. As you may know, your bank has a terrific reputation when it comes to investment advice."

Mrs. Allen will smile at you.

If you have a savings account at another bank, this is the time to transfer it into Mrs. Allen's bank. Remember, the more accounts you have here, the more attention you're going to get from Mrs. Allen.

If you're worried about losing a fraction of a percent of interest on your savings account with your transfer, don't. Of course, you do not want to break up some long-term savings arrangement and bring a lot of penalties down on your head. But if you have a regular savings account, and you like having some kind of small regular savings account for whatever reason—it makes you feel secure, or you don't understand or trust money market funds, or whatever—then give that small account to Mrs. Allen. If you do the arithmetic, most likely you'll find you'll be losing all of $25–$50 in interest a year. Beyond that, consider the value of what you'll be receiving in service and attention from Mrs. Allen.

Consider the dollar difference in your favor when it comes to loans. As we will see in Chapter 9, Mrs. Allen can make all the difference if you fall into a gray area on a loan. Your raw statistics might warrant a loan of $7,500. But with Mrs. Allen arguing your case and vouching for your dependability and your value as a customer, you will end up with the $10,000 you want.

How secretaries can get executive treatment

Secretaries can adapt much of the strategy I've been suggesting to their own special situation.

As one, you might not be earning big bucks, but you still can make yourself important to your bank. The way, like it or not, is through your boss. Use his leverage.

Ask him to do you a favor. Have him call the bank officer he deals with to get the "attention" process started.

I had a number of calls like that, and I was always happy to receive them. It was another chance for me to provide a special service for someone and in return get some special service for myself.

When the boss called, I'd always get the secretary on the phone, ask her to come in and talk. I couldn't care less if all she was earning was $10,000–$15,000. I treated her almost like Mrs. Jameson. I told her about the various services we had, suggested one or two she might be able to use and qualify for, like our credit card. I told her, if she ever had any trouble whatsoever with her account, even though it was only a Special Checking Account, she should call me, John Cook. "I'm a vice-president of this bank, Miss Drews, and I'm here to get rid of all your problems. Just think of me that way." And I meant it.

If she needed a loan, she probably needed my help. Because she was a woman, probably single, and not making much money, the scoring system in those days was rigged against her. But, I could often overrule the system.

Maybe once a year, I'd have her come into the bank for lunch. It was a big deal for her, and I knew it, but I also knew that I wanted her good will because I wanted her boss's good will, and this was one of the relatively easy ways I could nurture it. And I should add, those lunches were often just as pleasant or more so than any number of other lunches I endured with much fancier, financially fatter clients.

Furthermore, experience had taught me that often the only way to reach a top executive is through help from the secretary.

I had one situation where I was trying to sell a pension plan to a large corporation. It was a substantial plan, nicely suited to their needs, and placing it meant quite a lot to my record. I had sold all the junior staff on it. But I had to get it approved by the executive vice-president of the corporation. For four months I could not get the man on the phone, never mind meet with him. It was obvious to me that for whatever reasons, he didn't want to be involved in the program, but I kept plugging. It was also obvious that his secretary, though always as polite as she could be, had her orders.

For four months, I called once a week. Nothing. Then, one day, at the end of one of my calls, the secretary said: "Oh, by the way, Mr. Cook, I have a problem, and maybe you can straighten this out..." I nearly leapt through the phone.

She had a problem with the corporation's charitable gifts account. A silly but irritating thing having to do with the signature card on that account. Some dumb clerk was giving her a hard time.

Before the day was out, I had elicited the few relevant facts from the clerk, kept myself from strangling the man, and sent new signature cards over to my favorite secretary, by messenger. Whoosh. Her headache was gone.

She called the next day to thank me, and I told her I was delighted to help, which I most certainly was. I also told her that any time she ever had a problem, to call John Cook. "I'm your banker. Don't waste time with clerks, Mrs. Anthony, just give me a call. You people are important to me. Your company is very important to our bank, as you know, and your boss is terribly important to me, as I think you know."

"Oh, Mr. Cook, you're such a nice man. I'm sorry he hasn't been able to see you."

"Mrs. Anthony, I understand how busy he is. But if it would be possible to have a few minutes with him, it certainly would be wonderful."

"Let me see what I can do, Mr. Cook."

"Thank you so much, Mrs. Anthony. You're very kind."

Within one week, I had my meeting.

He bought our pension plan.

Special strategy for young people

Adapt the same "clout" strategy to your own particular circumstances and needs.

If you're moving to a new town, starting a job somewhere away from home, ask your parents for the favor. Have your mother or father or both, depending on their banking clout, call the officer they use at their bank.

Again, as it was with bosses calling on behalf of their secretaries. I received many calls from parents to help their children. Again, always welcome calls.

"My son has a job in Chicago, Mr. Cook, and I wonder if you could recommend a bank for him out there..."

Music to my ears. I'd make two calls.

First, to the officer in our bank who was in charge of our business in Chicago. He'd tell me exactly the person to call in Chicago and in exactly which of our correspondent banks.

In minutes, I have Christensen on the phone. "Our Mr. Jones suggested I might call you, Mr. Christensen. The son of one of our Preferred Customers is moving to Chicago, young fellow starting in a new job with the financial side of your Standard of Indiana out there. Don't know young Daniels myself, but his father keeps substantial balances with us. The family has been banking with us for years, they're Preferred Customers, Mr. Christensen, and I'd certainly appreciate any courtesies you might be able to extend to him."

"Mr. Cook, I'd be delighted to help. Please have him give me a call as soon as he hits town," Christensen replies, thinking happy thoughts. After all, I have just sent him a new and promising account, and who knows, it might even lead him into some of that incredibly juicy Standard of Indiana banking business.

But even if there were not all that much promise and glitter, my call would be just as effective. Whenever that young person arrived in the new town, there would be a banker to help. And, after all, starting a new job in a new city can be tough. Probably it's also the first time you're really away from home, living on your own. All help is welcome.

Instead of having some sour, indifferent person behind a banker's desk, my young people had a name and someone who knew their names and wanted to lend a hand.

That can make a great difference when, for example, they decide to buy their first car. They aren't worried about paying the loan off over thirty-six months, but what the standard car loan requirements might be. Those might require an applicant to have worked in a job for, say, six months. Maybe my young people have been in the new job only three months.

If they didn't have my Mr. Christensen, they'd fill out the form, have it scored by the computer, and they wouldn't get the loan. But with Christensen in their lives, it's a simple matter. They go to him, tell him they're a big boy or girl now, want their own car. He's not a computer. He knows what the computer doesn't know—that they have come to him because he got called by me, and I care about them and their family, and so should he.

Congratulations. You just bought your first car.

Everyone in his first job suffers the shocks of the real world. You took Economics 101, but nothing ever prepared you for, say, taxes. Your job is supposed to pay you $200 a week, $300 a week. Whatever the amount, it seems a fortune to you.

Then, suddenly, it isn't there. Something about all this money they take out each week for taxes, for social security, maybe for a pension plan, union dues. So that $200–$300 melts down to $150–$250.

But in your head, you're still making the fortune. For all kinds of fascinating reasons, you don't make the adjustment. The result is, about six months out into the real world, you get this warning from the phone company that they are going to disconnect.

You are outraged, of course, for being treated like some common criminal. But something tells you it is better to pay the bill than take them to the Supreme Court. You need a quick $500, and the place to get it, like it or not, is from home.

Happens to everyone. And once again, your life will

brighten, thanks to me and Mr. Christensen. With us on your side, there'll be no hysterical delays from the U.S. Postal Service. You won't have to stave off the dreaded phone company for seven long days. Nor will there be any grubby inconvenience for your parents, who might otherwise have to withdraw the money from their account, take the cash to some bleak Western Union office.

Your parents simply call me. I have the $500 transferred that same day from their account to yours in Mr. Christensen's bank.

A few buttons punched, and swoosh... now your headache is also gone.

Checklist:

Getting service out of your old bank, at last

1. Dig out the officer in charge of your account.
2. Have a meeting to review your past and very bright future.
3. Think of yourself as a small business (or a steamy Less Developed Country).
4. Sign up for services, even if you don't need them.
5. Special advice for secretaries: Use your boss's clout.
6. Special advice for young people: Use your parents' clout.

Chapter 6

Fancy stuff: savings and investment "instruments"

There used to be magic in the initials "CD." It stood for a certificate of deposit, and it used to be a form of savings available to someone who had a loose $100,000 sitting around. The bank, in effect, told those people that if they had nothing better to do with their money for some months, they could lend the $100,000 to the bank, and receive, not the paltry interest of a savings account, but several points higher, guaranteed.

In the days when a savings account was paying 5 percent interest, that could be an interesting, safe use of money for a reasonably short period of time. In the trust department, we always considered CD's good things to include in a portfolio, an anchor against more risky common stocks.

Then in recent years, my friends in the marketing side of banking got the wonderful idea that they could do something with the cachet of those classy initials. Suddenly, banks everywhere were offering what they called "CD's," only you didn't need $100,000; often you didn't need $10,000.

In fact, these weren't real "CD's," they were simply "time deposits" in a fancy wrapping. You gave the bank your money, usually a minimum of $3,000, and left it with them for a year, eighteen months, twenty-four months, thirty-six months, however long they could lure you in, and they gave you higher than the going interest rate for savings.

Were these good things, these new "instruments"? Were they a form of savings, or investment? How's a person to know, how's a person to sort all these new things out?

In the area of "instruments," there's always been a fair amount of confusion among average people because banks never much told them what was available to them. With the recent rash of apparently new "instruments," the confusion is compounded by all the claims and advertising. Again, we're in the automobile showroom, even if it has marble columns.

Let me try to sort out some of this, so that we can see if banks are really offering anything new, anything that's better for you. And let's also consider some basic questions that always confused my banking customers.

Two key questions to ask yourself

Forget the ads, forget the banks. Start by thinking of your own needs.

One of the biggest problems I had with my customers was getting them to understand the difference between money they wanted to save and money they wanted to invest.

The whole idea of saving has been eroded over the years. Even into the mid-1960s, people still thought in terms of putting a certain percentage of their earnings into savings. It had to be there for emergencies. If you lost your job, you knew you could survive without having to sell your house until you could find another job. Simple, remember?

And, if you also remember, the amount of interest you earned on those savings was a secondary consideration. What mattered was that you knew the money was there, absolutely safe, and that you could get your hands on it the day you needed it.

These days, we all know that attitudes toward savings have changed radically. Inflation makes it much tougher to save. There are also interesting alternatives to traditional savings accounts, like money market funds and the new high interest rate accounts that banks are now permitted to offer. But most of all, the change, I think, stems from the idea of "easy money."

If I believed all the stories I heard in the 1960s about killings in the market, I'd also have to believe that there is a glut of millionaires in America today. Not only Wall Street friends, bank associates, and fancy business customers, but very plain guys who commuted with me from New Jersey. Everybody was becoming a millionaire overnight, and not only that, they were doing it with almost no capital.

Well, we all know about those stocks that went from 8 to 180 and back down to 1⅛, and I know that those same guys are still commuting with me and not out sailing their yachts.

But the idea didn't die with those go-go stocks. Once it's been done, the possibility exists that it can happen again. "Make your money work for you..." the ads from Wall Street and from your bank tell you, and heaven knows, there's sense in that. Of course, you want to make your money work for you but the trick is to do it in the way that best suits your real needs.

All I saw, as the fallout of this "easy money" syndrome, was greed and stupidity, and it came from the nicest of people.

One day, a man came into the bank waving *The Wall Street Journal* at me. He had just started reading this incredible paper, he admitted, and look here. He pointed at a new bond issue from AT&T. They were offering 13 percent interest, which was 8 percent more than he was getting from his savings account, guaranteed for thirty years. "I'd be a fool not to move my money into that."

"Maybe so, maybe not," I told him. "First, answer me two questions. How much do you want to save? How much do you want to invest?"

"What do you mean?"

"If you move your money into the AT&T bonds, you're no longer saving. You're now investing."

"C'mon, you call that investing? A guaranteed return of 13 percent for thirty years? I call that stealing."

"How much you got in your savings account right now?"

"About $20,000."

"So, you'd put all your money into bonds? Have nothing left in savings?"

"Mr. Cook, I don't want to rub this in, but I'd still be saving. Only I'd be saving with AT&T."

I knew the man, and I knew he lived on his earnings. "Mr. Dannon, what happens if you lose your job in six months? Nothing in your savings account?"

"Sell my bonds."

"If there's a buyer. There are times when there are no buyers in the bond market. None. Or, maybe you find a buyer, but the market price of that bond has dropped so you lose $7,000 of your $20,000. Hardly impossible, Mr. Dannon, hardly farfetched at all. It's taken you years and years to save $20,000, and you blow more than a third of it in a matter of months."

"With all due respect, Mr. Cook, I think you just want to keep my $20,000 in your bank."

"Do as you please, Mr. Dannon, but if you buy those bonds, you should have your head examined, if you'll pardon my frankness."

He paused. "Well, what should I do? I can't sit around and be ripped off by your bank, if you'll pardon *my* frankness."

Happily, we were back at square one, where we

could consider what the man really needed. In fact, we figured out that he didn't need all $20,000 sitting in that savings account. If he got fired from his job, he would collect severance pay, and if necessary, he could sell some common stock. Certainly, with those, he could handle six months with nothing coming in if he also had $10,000 to draw on from the savings account.

So, we found a nice compromise. We left $10,000 in the savings account, withdrew the other $10,000, and in a slightly complicated maneuver, I put that together with some similar amounts from other customers and bought them commercial paper, of which more later in this chapter. The great advantage of that to Dannon was that he had a quite safe investment, which in that case would pay him more than his savings account but tie up his money for only ninety days. (Lest you wonder, this all happened before there were high interest rate accounts or money market funds, as we now know them.)

Even more important, so far as I was concerned, I had a customer who had begun to see the difference between savings and investments. He had begun to see that with one he could have the money available to him at any time; with the other, he had to find a buyer in the marketplace. With one, he had no risk; with the other, considerable risk.

With his savings account, it didn't matter to him if the stock market went down, interest rates went up, the federal government was going to increase its debt— all conditions that would affect his investment. They would not directly affect his savings account or its interest.

At certain levels of savings, and at certain times, he would have to be concerned about the effect of inflation on his money. But that can be handled, partly by limiting the amounts of savings, as I did with Dannon, and under certain conditions by moving excess money into the new money market funds, or the new variable rate high interest accounts in your bank.

Their great advantage over a regular savings account is that they do pay so much more interest. I am not contradicting the earlier point I made—that interest is a secondary consideration when it comes to savings. It is. But, today, we are forced to adjust for inflation.

If inflation runs 10 percent a year, and you are receiving only 5½ percent on your savings, the true value of your savings is actually diminishing by 4½ percent (your interest, less the amount of inflation).

If however, your interest is running about 12 percent a year, the value of your money is protected and growing by 2 percent (your interest, less the 10 percent rate of inflation).

How much? How liquid?

Saving money is tough today, though I still recommend putting aside 10 percent of what you earn. The best way to do it is through some forced savings plan, where your company takes a set percentage out of your paycheck. If your company doesn't offer such a plan, see if your bank doesn't have one with which they automatically move a certain amount from your checking account into your savings account each month.

People used to come to me having saved $1,000, and they thought they'd reached a magical peak where something had to be done with their little fortune. Again, the ads, the temptations, the gossip of "easy money."

I told them they had no problem, just leave it in their savings account. For now, that's their rock.

Well, they'd ask, what about moving it from the bank I'm in, where I'm only getting 5¼ percent interest, to one where I can get 5½ percent? Whereupon I would offer them a moment of revelation. I'd point out that the annual difference in interest would be $3.44, period. (With the new law, people won't even have to worry themselves sick over that $3.44. It eliminates that small difference and small advantage savings institutions had been granted over commercial banks.)

People went on and on about interest rates on savings accounts, but they never did the arithmetic. If you had $5,000 in a savings account at 5¼ percent, at the end of a year you'd have $5,269.50. If you changed banks and went up to 5½ percent interest, at the end of the year you'd have $5,286.71, a difference of a huge $17.21.

When it comes to savings accounts, I tell people to put their money in and forget about the interest. You aren't using the money as an investment, to make you more money; you're using it as savings, to bring you security. Forget about the interest.

There are other, more important reasons than a few extra dollars in interest for choosing a bank for your savings account. Clout, for example. The more business you give your primary bank, the more service they'll give you. Or, a future mortgage. Looking ahead, you can see the day when you'll want to buy instead of rent. Your local savings bank might be the best place to get that mortgage, and they'll only give it to you if you're a customer. So keep a savings account with them.

More interest? How liquid?

There are countless new plans that offer higher interest rates—many of these, as I noted, are now being called "CD's."

And just as the ads say, they will indeed pay you more for your money.

But they require you to leave your money with the bank for long, predetermined stretches of time, six months, two and a half years, whatever. If you need that money before the time is up, you can usually get it back, but with severe penalties. With a six-month plan, a normal penalty would force you to forfeit three months of the interest you've earned, for any early withdrawal. Make that six months interest forfeited with a two-and-a-half-year plan. Which means that you end up worse off than if you had your money in a regular savings account.

Again, you're trading a shot at some extra interest for total liquidity, which is to say, for total availability of your savings. To decide, first ask yourself if you're sure you won't need the money for six months, two years, or however long the plan is. If that's so, then ask yourself, is that the best place you can put your money?

There are four other financial "instruments" your bank has available that are worth considering, even though only one of them, Treasury bills, may be of potential use to you. In addition to Treasury bills, I have in mind bonds, commercial paper, and certificates of deposit.

The practicality of each really depends on your answers to two questions, which are variations on our earlier basic questions: To save? Or, to invest?

Now you should ask yourself: How much money do I have? How long do I want to tie it up?

Each of these "instruments" requires your commitment to tie up a significant amount of money for a set period of time. Can you afford to put that money aside for that length of time? With each, if you change your mind and take your money out early, before the maturity date, in one way or another, you can end up paying dearly.

Treasury Bills

This is an I.O.U. from the government. It is one of the techniques the government uses to borrow money on a short-term basis, for a year or less. The bills are issued for periods of 90, 180, and 360 days, and the least you may buy is $10,000. (They differ from other Treasury securities you might have heard of, in their short maturity periods. Treasury notes mature in anything from a year to ten years, and Treasury bonds cover anything ten years and longer.)

You may buy these through your bank, but banks in general don't want to bother with the things, since there's no real profit in it for them. No big ad campaigns announcing "T-bills... yet another nifty thing you can pick up from your friendly banker." Providing them for rich folks is another matter. For them, your bank probably won't even charge a fee for handling the transaction.

For you, expect to pay about $25 for the transaction of the purchase. If you sell it, before it matures, of which more in a moment, they'll charge you a second $25 fee. There is paperwork and somebody's time involved, but the real reason for the fees is to discourage you from buying the things and bothering them. Don't be put off. T-bills can be extremely useful to you and well worth the fees.

If you don't want to buy them through your bank, a stockbroker can do it for you, or you can buy them directly from your district Federal Reserve Bank, if you want to spend the time doing it. One-year bills go on sale every fourth Thursday, and the rest, every Monday. You can buy them right at your Fed, or they can tell you how to do it through the mail.

A T-bill is what is known as a "discounted investment," which is to say your earnings are calculated into your purchase price, and you buy at a "discounted" price. So, if you are buying a note for $10,000 and the government that day is going to pay you 10 percent for your money, you give them a check for only $9,000 (the full value of the note, $10,000, less the amount you'll earn). Then, at the end of 360 days, the government sends you a check for the full $10,000.

Under certain circumstances, they are excellent savings vehicles. They are not excellent investment vehicles, or even, to my way of thinking, investments at all. Again, back when I was managing trusts, I would often take that portion of the trust that we did not want to invest, and put it into T-bills. Completely secure, and with the trusts, we know we probably wouldn't have to touch them before they matured.

Many people these days who don't have trusts or big buck investment portfolios use T-bills in a similar way: They're a safe harbor for cash; an alternative to money market funds; returning an amount that will beat the rate of inflation and so preserve capital, plus a bit more in the name of profit. Also, your earnings on them cannot be taxed by state or local governments, a benefit you don't have with money market earnings. T-bill earnings are taxed, however, by the federal government, treated as ordinary income.

They are also quite liquid. If you buy a T-bill for 360 days and six months later an emergency arises and you need your $9,000, you can sell your note immediately. You won't pay any automatic penalty, either, as you would with a typical time deposit savings plan.

However, the amount you receive, over and above your $9,000 investment, depends completely on the marketplace. If the rate has gone up since you bought at 10 percent, and it's now at 15 percent, the total amount you'll collect is $9,250. The person who buys your T-bill benefits from the higher rate, not you. He gets that new rate of 15 percent and that has to be figured into your sale price.

In this case, he would be earning $750, and that amount deducted from the $10,000 value of the note at maturity leaves you with $9,250.

To be sure, you still have your basic nut, and you can cover your emergency needs. But $250 earned over six months on your money means you earned only 5 percent. Plus, if you bought and sold through your bank, you may have to pay two transaction fees, which will bring your rate down to around 4 percent.

If I'd had any sense that maybe you'd need your nut before a full 360 days was up, you might have bought the T-bill for a shorter period, say, for 90 days. But then your earnings would be less than you'd get for a full year. If the feds were paying 10 percent for a year's loan, maybe they'd give you only 8 percent on ninety days. At that rate, you'd earn $200 and still have the buy and sell fees to pay.

As I said: How much? And how long?

Bonds

You can get these through your bank, but unless you are very rich and you don't like brokers—which is where you ought to buy them—they don't make much sense.

At first, I was puzzled that people actually came to me at the bank, wanting to buy a bond. Then I realized two things: First, they liked the very idea of bonds. They envisioned themselves "clipping coupons," just as J. P. Morgan used to do. In fact, the practice is dying out. It used to be that when interest on a bond came due, J. P. and his friends clipped a coupon attached to the bond, turned it in to their bank, and got the money due them. Today, more and more companies are issuing bonds without the coupons, and when interest payments are due, the company's computers automatically churn out checks that are mailed to bondholders.

The second thing I realized was that these people really knew next to nothing about bonds—like Mr. Dannon who came in waving his *Wall Street Journal* at me, thinking his AT&T bond was simply a better kind of savings account.

Generally speaking, you'll need $10,000 to get into bonds, and when you buy at that level, you are a nuisance. You're a nuisance to your bank; you're a nuisance to the whole market. Bonds are, after all, huge promissory notes issued by giant corporations, or maybe cities or utility companies, attempting to borrow great sums for long periods of time, typically twenty to thirty years. They don't want to bother with your measly ten grand. So the fees for handling the crummy sale are going to be high, and if you go to dump the bond, you're going to be delayed with settlement requirements and hit with other fees.

That's assuming, of course, that you can sell the bond at all. A facet of the general ignorance about bonds is the belief that they're as liquid as common stocks. They aren't. At certain bad times, you can't sell your bond to anyone. And, as I told Mr. Dannon, even if you find a buyer, you risk selling at a great loss. That used to shock people, when I'd warn them, because they thought bonds were so totally safe.

As you might have gathered, I used to try to talk most people out of the whole idea of bonds, especially if they intended to buy them with their savings.

Bonds can and often do make sense as part of a balanced investment package, and tax-free bonds can be a critical instrument in the financial planning of someone in the 50 percent federal tax bracket. But that's hardly what Mr. Dannon had in mind.

Commercial Paper

This is another form of corporate I.O.U., but unlike bonds, these loans are for short stretches, anything up to about a year.

Again, in small amounts they are a pain in the neck to your bank, so you don't see these instruments advertised. But they might suit your purposes. They can pay the highest interest rates available for short terms.

Like bonds, they are meant to be traded in substantial amounts, millions of dollars. So for your bank to get involved at all, it has to put together enough to make sense.

Minimum amounts vary. The Bank of the Southwest in Houston in 1982 would let you buy thirty-day or ninety-day paper with a minimum purchase of $25,000. Manufacturers Hanover Trust Company in New York, at the same time, required $30,000 from you. Wells Fargo in San Francisco had a $25,000 minimum.

At The Bank of New York we didn't have established minimums, so I made my own rules for my own customers. There were about twenty of them who told me they wanted to buy commercial paper, and they gave me the authority to do it for them, to take a certain amount out of their accounts and buy it when it was available.

I'd put together a package in amounts that varied from about $10,000 to $25,000, and with $150,000 to $200,000 in our kitty, I'd call our money desk and tell them to buy the paper. The total made the transaction reasonable for the bank, and by breaking it down into small chunks, I offered something special and cemented my working relationships with twenty good customers.

All major corporations borrow this way, and their paper is rated according to their credit worthiness. Those with the highest ratings, as you'd expect, can sell their paper at lower interest rates than corporations in which the risk is considered greater.

And there is risk. You are, after all, lending money to a corporation, with no guarantees from the bank, the government, or anyone that you're going to be paid back. If the company collapses, goes bankrupt, yours is about the last debt that will be honored.

It can happen. The memory of Penn Central is fresh in my mind. They would never go belly-up, I heard all my banking friends say, over and over and over again, as if wishing would make it so. They talked themselves into it, right up to the terrible end—and it was swift in coming, as it always is, here today, gone tomorrow. Right up to the very end, Penn Central was selling commercial paper to banks and insurance companies and all kinds of financial institutions that, of course, knew everything was going to turn out all right.

The real Certificates of Deposit

The mother of all time deposits, the CD traditionally was a deposit of at least $100,000 for a set period, usually thirty to ninety days, on which the bank would pay its highest interest. The interest was regulated, and so was the volume a given bank could maintain, but for both bank and rich person, this was and is a useful short-term instrument.

Completely insured up to $100,000, it offers the safest way to harbor cash at a time when you don't want to put it into the market, say, because you don't like present developments.

As opposed to the other instruments we've been considering in this chapter, your bank will be only too happy to tell you all about this one and accommodate you and your homeless, neglected $100,000.

So far as the marketing geniuses are concerned, I think we've pretty well come full cycle now on this one. I was delighted to learn recently that the Pan American Bank in Miami now offers something called a "Regular CD," for which they require only $1,000 of your money. And just so you keep things in perspective, they also offer something with the wonderful name of "Jumbo CD." And how much do you have to give them for that whopper of a "Jumbo"? Why, $100,000, of course.

Chapter 7

Credit:
Creating it,
building it,
protecting it

While the personal connection with your banker is essential, it alone is not enough. Your banker can love you very much, really enjoy your company, but before he or she can do anything for you in the way of a loan, you've got to have credit.

Let's take a look at how to get it, improve it, and protect it.

When you go in for a loan, your bank officer will have two immediate questions in mind.

1. Do you really want to pay him back, or are you, underneath that smile and those nice clothes, a crook?

2. Can you, are you able to pay him back, even if you have all the desire in the world to do so?

A check on your credit goes a long way toward answering those questions.

I have had any number of customers get offended by credit checks. "I've been banking here for years," they tell me. That's true, but I don't know what else they've been doing.

In our own bank, there never used to be credit checks on loans for vice-presidents and above. Then a vice-president of a large New York bank got in trouble with a loan he had at another bank, and they sued him to collect on it. Needless to say, everyone in the New York banking world heard the news, and it was hardly surprising that soon after, our bank along with many others established a new policy: everyone had to undergo the normal credit check. One result of this was that one of our top officers was turned down for a loan by his own bank.

The five main steps to establishing credit

1. *Open a checking account.* If you don't have one, a banker gets suspicious.

I've known people earning $30,000, $40,000, and they were too cheap to pay the monthly service charges on a checking account. But a banker wonders with such people, if he's dealing with a crackpot. Maybe this nut will decide at some point that the interest is too high and stop paying it.

A checking account gives you a credential. And if the bank wants to verify it, see how you handle it, it can. Mortgage banks will check you out on that one, see what kinds of balance you maintain. Most other banks don't even bother. It's enough for them to know that you're already part of the banking world.

When a potential creditor does check, by the way, what they want and what your bank tells them is your average balance. "It's in the low three figures..." "It's in the high four figures..." Nobody deals in the exact amount you have in the account at that moment, because that could be an aberration. You could slip an extra $5,000 in there for a few days to make a good impression. The potential creditor wants a long-term feel.

2. *Open charge accounts, lots of them.* Department stores are the easiest places to get charge accounts because they know just how directly their sales are tied to charging.

Get as many accounts as you can, and use them. Obviously, you also have to use self-control here. But, if you need furniture, or clothes, don't wait until you've saved the money. Open a charge account, buy the stuff, and then pay it off according to the terms, exactly and religiously.

If you can do that, you show a bank that, in fact, when you have a loan, you pay it back.

3. *Consider making your first loan elsewhere.* To establish credit, in the end you have to get someone to lend you money. The Catch-22 is that no one wants to be first. Your bank would consider being second, but it would feel even better about being fourth or fifth.

The way to cope is to go to one of those lending companies who are more willing than a bank to take a chance on you.

Places like CIT, Beneficial Finance, and Household Finance all got started, in fact, by lending money to people whom banks were scared of. CIT, for example, has developed a very large business by trusting Puerto Ricans who live on the island. Indeed, CIT found that those Puerto Rican natives, whom the big banks turned aside, were fanatically responsible when it came to repaying loans.

These companies charge a bit more than banks, since their risks and costs are higher than those of banks. But it could be worth it to you.

Before going to one of them, talk with your banker, and ask him whether you'd have trouble getting your $1,000 loan from the bank. Tell him it's your first loan, you haven't had your job all that long, and whatever else you think might count against you. If he advises you that your chances are not so good, don't risk it. You don't want a loan rejection on your record, before you've even started.

Instead, go to one of the private loan companies. And, as you did with the department stores, figure out how much you can afford to pay back and borrow up to your limit.

Again, don't go crazy. Borrow what you know you can handle, and pay it back just as quickly and comfortably as you can. If you can pay it back before it's due, you have put something on your record that looks very good to any banker. Not only have you met your obligation, fast, but you show him that you are planning. You borrowed $1,000, but when your cash situation improved a bit and you could pay it back faster than anticipated, that's what you did. You didn't simply take the extra cash and inflate your lifestyle. Bankers love that.

4. *Consider making your first loan from your company's credit bureau.* Often you'll find the best terms and the easiest credit requirements with company credit bureaus. So check them out first.

The amounts they lend are usually lower than banks or private lending companies, but it might be enough to cover your early needs.

And, most important, a loan taken and repaid to them will show a banker that you have been through the process at least once.

5. *Find a cosigner.* This is fairly common for young people. They get a parent to cosign a loan with them.

The bank is extending the loan on the strength of the parent's credit, and the parent is just as liable as the son or daughter to pay the thing off.

One important point, if you use a cosigner: Be very careful that you yourself pay off the loan, and on time. If a bank officer sees that you had such a loan but your parent had to bail you out, you get two black marks.

First, the bank officer will think you simply are not

able to handle payments. Second, he'll figure that you also deceived your parent when you got him to sign for the loan.

But, if you take such a loan and handle it well, you'll have a track record of doing good loan business.

Your place in the great credit galaxy

Once you establish credit and are officially born into the credit world, your actions in that world are tracked monthly, until you die, or drop out of the credit world, which for most people is the same thing.

The way you handle that first loan, the way you pay off those first charge accounts, and all your subsequent loans and charge accounts are reported to one of the four or five major national credit organizations: TRW, CBI, Transamerica, Chilton, or Pinger.

At The Bank of New York we used TRW Information Services, the largest of them. They have been in the credit service business since the mid-1960s, which is when the credit business became automated with electronic computers. Before then, reporting was done on a more local basis, all of it manually.

Now TRW has about 40,000 banks, retail stores, finance companies, and credit card companies feeding it information every month about you and the way you're conducting your business.

If you're sixty days late paying Hudson's department store, or you're ninety days late with your car payments, or you're behind on your bank loan, each of those places sends that damaging information to TRW every month. If you're paying everything on time, that also gets sent. The full picture is what they're after.

Beyond all that data, they cover the courts, collecting every lien, judgment, or bankruptcy that's placed against you. They used to record every suit against you, but have come to realize that a suit is only an allegation until resolved otherwise.

TRW stores this data on you in its computer banks in Anaheim, California. They're tracking 86 million people out there. The information they store is second in volume only to the Social Security data banks.

Every time you go to your bank for a loan, or apply for a charge account or a credit card, all the potential lender has to do to find out about you is punch a few keys.

Those keys, whether they are part of a teleprinter system or a computer that is connected directly with TRW computers in Anaheim, sends the request. "Cook, Joh, SS# 2954860338."

That's all Anaheim needs to know. Who I am, my last name, the first three letters of my first name, my Social Security number. Though the computer doesn't need the reason for the inquiry, a bank will add it; in this case, I'm applying for a consumer installment loan, to be paid off in thirty-six months, in the amount of $10,000.

That last data is for other banks to see, in case I try to hit several banks in one day, figuring that before they can possibly learn that I'm applying simultaneously to all of them, I'll collect $10,000 from one, $10,000 from another down the block, $10,000 more from one on the way to the airport, all of which will give me a nice start on my new life in Rio.

The Anaheim computer gets your request, retrieves every piece of information it has stored away on you, and transmits your complete credit profile back to the bank.

That entire process, from inquiry to the time the bank starts to receive your credit report, takes approximately seven seconds.

The report comes through the bank's computer or teleprinter, usually about one and a half to two pages for an individual, neatly typed out in three colors, columns of red, white, and blue.

As you can see from the sample we have here, the thing is fairly impressive in its completeness. The loans you're carrying, and how you're doing. Even loans you applied for and didn't get. The charge accounts you're using, and how you're doing. The court actions against you.

The TRW computer has an adjustable memory. Bankruptcies are shown for ten years from the time they were adjudicated. Any other kind of black mark, if you are late, or not paying according to terms, or suffering tax liens, is carried for seven years. Good news—how you are managing open accounts and current loans as you are supposed to—is carried indefinitely.

It all sounds neat, clean, swift, perfect. Except we all know the world doesn't work that way.

How to protect your credit report

What TRW has in those data banks is what your creditors tell them about you. There is no guarantee at all that their information is correct, and until recently there wasn't much you could do to protect yourself. Now, thanks to new federal credit protection laws, there is a lot you can do, and must.

First, if your loan application gets rejected, press your banker for a reason. Don't let him get away with the old dodge: "Sorry, the loan committee wouldn't approve this one." *There is no loan committee*. Nor is there any "banking committee" with its "applicable loan policies."

Ask him directly, if one of the reasons relates to your credit report. There is no law that requires him to tell you the truth, but if he answers yes, there is a law that requires him to tell you which credit company the bank used.

You then have the further right by law to contact that credit company and get the same credit report they issued to your bank, free of charge.

Once you have the report, you can see for yourself what turned the bank against you. And if the damaging information is false or erroneous, you can get it corrected.

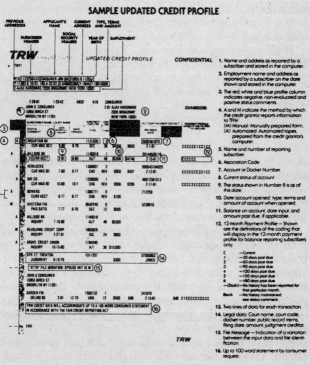

SAMPLE UPDATED CREDIT PROFILE

TRW CREDIT DATA — EASTERN REGION

1. Name and address as reported by a subscriber and stored in the computer.

2. Employment name and address as reported by a subscriber on the date shown and stored in the computer.

3. The red, white and blue profile column indicates negative, non-evaluated and positive status comments.

4. A and M indicate the method by which the credit grantor reports information to TRW.
   (M) Manual: Manually prepared form.
   (A) Automated: Automated tapes, prepared from the credit grantor's computer.

5. Name and number of reporting subscriber.

6. Association Code.

7. Account or Docket Number.

8. Current status of account.

9. The status shown in Number 8 is as of this date.

10. Date account opened; type, terms and amount of account when opened.

11. Balance on account, date input, and amount past due, if applicable.

12. 12-Month Payment Profile — Shown are the definitions of the coding that will display in the 12-month payment profile for balance reporting subscribers only.

C	—Current
1	—30 days past due
2	—60 days past due
3	—90 days past due
4	—120 days past due
5	—150 days past due
6	—180 days past due
—(Dash)	—No history has been reported for that particular month.
Blank	—No history maintained: see status comment.

13. Two lines of data for each transaction.

14. Legal data: Court name, court code, docket number, public record items, filing date, amount, judgment creditor.

15. File Message — Indication of a variation between the input data and file identification.

16. Up to 100 word statement by consumer request.

IMPORTANT: Use of this information is governed by the terms and conditions of the subscriber agreement. NOTE: It is possible that all of the above information may not pertain to the individuals inquired upon unless otherwise noted. Employment shown on the report are as reported by subscribers.

TRW CREDIT DATA a division of TRW Inc.

1821/108 E
Rev. 4/81

Let's suppose you had a problem with a Boston department store.

First, you go back to TRW or the appropriate credit company: "You've got me delinquent ninety days on payment of a sofa. Filene's department store in Boston. I never accepted delivery of that sofa, two of the legs were broken. They took the sofa back, but there was some clerical error. They billed me for three months, before I could get them to credit me the $700 instead of billing me."

TRW then writes to Filene's. "Is that true?" they ask. Filene's has fifteen days to respond, and if they don't, the black mark is electronically erased.

Chances are, Filene's will get back to TRW, and they might very well say, "We think we were right, but we'll review it with the customer."

You then inform TRW: "I want to tell my side of this story." And they'll let you. They'll give you a paragraph of up to 100 words to add to the bottom of your credit report. They won't let you libel Filene's, but at least you can make clear to your bank or anyone else thinking of giving you credit that you were sold a busted sofa, and you are disputing the whole charge.

You then go to Filene's directly and show them your records, letters, notes, whatever you have to prove your case. They look the stuff over and say: "Sorry, you're right after all," and they inform TRW. They correct your profile, and at your request, they'll send the proud, new report to anyone who had asked for one on you during the previous year, which includes, of course, your bank.

At that point, you should go back to your bank officer, review your new TRW report with him, and ask for his guidance. Could you, with the corrected report, now qualify for the loan?

As a banker, I found myself in that position several times. I always told people the real reason their loan applications were rejected, and if it was because of trouble they'd had with credit, questionable trouble, I told them how to clear their record and encouraged them to come back to me once they had.

When they did return, I was especially sympathetic to their case and pushed hard to get them the loan. Understandably, I first had to surmount their fury. They had been made to suffer, inconvenienced, embarrassed, all because of some store's inefficiency.

Their good name had been temporarily ruined because of some clerk's error.

That's true. In the credit world, you are guilty until you prove yourself innocent. And even when the charge against you is erroneous, you still must disprove it.

All unfair and infuriating. But I can only tell you what I told my customers. It is much better than it used to be. The wrongs can be corrected. And until a federal law forces still greater responsibility on the part of the reporting creditors, there is the chance that your credit will be damaged by mistake.

The chance, I should add, is not all that great. You should not imagine that gremlins are lurking in the TRW data banks. You should not fear, every time you apply for some credit, that you are doomed to be ensnared in battle against an invisible enemy. But if you are victimized that way, be prepared to endure the hassle and clear your record. Justly or not, it's the only way you can reestablish your proper credit standing.

If trouble hits, unexpectedly

Speaking of credit and trouble, here's another piece of advice.

Let's suppose you got the loan, $10,000, and you have three years to pay it off. Everything is fine for a year, then you lose your job.

That happens all the time. Suddenly, you are strapped and cannot afford the $377 a month, which you had been sending in faithfully. Unfortunately, most people faced with that problem panic. They simply stop paying, and in doing so, they immediately damage their credit. The news that they are not paying according to terms is bleeped monthly to credit bureaus everywhere.

What you should do in a tough situation like that is simple: Go in and tell them what's happened. Your banker has seen and heard that before. He will restructure your loan. Spread it out to four years, perhaps, and lower your monthly payments from $377 to $208.

Even then, if you hit a stretch where you can't put together the $208, send something, send $50. That won't hurt you with the bank. You're in a "workout loan situation," and the bank expects that one way or another, that's exactly what you'll do, "work it out."

But if they don't hear anything from you, and you are simply delinquent on your payments, you damage your credit profile, and your relationship with your bank.

Another piece of advice: Before you go in for a loan, get your credit profile and study it.

In the coming chapters, we'll consider the whole loan process, and exactly what you should do to get the loan you're after. You'll see then how your credit report is one of four major considerations in determining whether or not you get the loan.

If you have any question about your credit, any memory of a credit problem within the last seven to ten years, you'd be wise to ask your bank officer, long before you go to see him for the loan, which credit bureau the bank uses. It might be more than one, since some banks combine the data from a national company with that from a more local operation.

Then contact them and get the profile or profiles on yourself. As we'll see, what you learn from those reports can be strategic information for you to pass along to your bank officer, before he discovers it for himself, or hears about it in a surprise call from one of the bank's credit reviewers.

The laws that give you a fighting chance

Nearly everyone is ambivalent about credit. We view it warmly when it allows us to borrow needed money and open charge accounts that make life easier.

It also makes us crazy with worry that, for reasons sound or uncontrollable, it can go sour, render us lepers, shower us with pain and frustration.

What you should understand is that the credit monster is controllable. So many customers have come to me for loans with the lurking fear that they won't get the loan because there is something they don't know about, some dreadful black act recorded in their secret credit file. As we have seen, there are ways to control such things from happening to you.

These same people compound their anxiety. If by some miracle I should get the loan, they say to themselves, something will happen to me, and I won't be able to keep up the payments, and then they'll come and get me. They'll cause me to lose my job. Take away my car. Take away my house. Put me in jail. The electric chair.

Well, if you get into credit trouble, there are laws intended to let you sleep at night and protect you from the electric chair. I am thinking especially of the federal consumer laws enacted since the late 1960s.

I can tell you that these laws and regulations are taken very seriously by banks, credit companies, department stores, car dealers, retailers of all kinds, anyone offering credit to you. For the most part, they are also taken seriously today by collection companies. The laws are enforced; the penalties are real. In recent years, most state governments have become vigilant in protecting consumers in general and their credit rights in particular. The combination of federal law and state action has made an enormous difference in a short time. (In the Appendix of this book, you'll find a listing of places to turn to if you think your rights have been violated.)

Let's consider four of the laws that are especially relevant to us.

Truth in Lending Act

This requires banks or other lenders to make clear how much a loan is going to cost you in interest, both in dollars and as an annual percentage rate.

It used to be common practice, especially for small finance companies, to confuse borrowers with "discounted loans." The interest would be taken off the top of the loan, but the borrower would still have to pay back the full amount of the loan, even though he never got to use all the money. All he ended up with was the full amount, minus the total interest. In cases like that, the real interest rate might actually be closer to 30 percent, rather than the 15 percent the company might pretend it is.

The law also requires lenders to be specific about the repayment plan. They must state exactly when you are expected to pay, how often, for how long.

Again, eliminate doubt and confusion.

The Fair Credit Reporting Act

It used to be that you could barely gain access to your own credit file. Or find out why you had been denied credit or a loan. If you were able to get some information and discovered errors, it was practically impossible for you to do anything about it.

This law changes all that; it gives you the right to know what's in any credit report on you, know why you're having trouble getting credit, and to correct anything in your report that needs it.

To a limited degree, it also prevents credit bureaus from selling your credit file to anyone who asks. In theory, they can sell your information to anyone who is deciding whether or not to give you credit; or, anyone who is thinking about hiring you; or, for insurance purposes.

Those, plus one other category, which is something of a loophole: Where there is a "legitimate business need for the information in connection with a business transaction involving" you. Which is how, without applying for it, you can receive in the mail an invitation from a bank or a credit card company to sign on the dotted line and find yourself with an immediate new line of credit for $1,500, or whatever.

Still, this law has definitely helped to create a new atmosphere in the credit world. Credit companies today are much more careful about your rights and how they respond to you than they were before this act was passed in 1970.

Equal Credit Opportunity Act

In Chapter 12, "Who They Really Are," we'll take a look at bankers at their worst. The Equal Credit Opportunity Act effectively pushes them to treat everyone the same, even though they don't believe that people are equal, or deserve evenhanded treatment.

What it says is regardless of race, religion, age, sex, or marital status, Mr. Banker, consider their loan application as you would an application from someone you approve of.

To a large degree, the law works. Loans to women, especially divorced women, were considered absolutely foolhardy, just twenty years ago. Now the law prohibits a banker from discriminating against a woman, or under most circumstances from even asking a woman, or a man for that matter, if she or he is married, or divorced, or separated. As we'll see in Chapter 8, you don't even have to tell your bank on a loan application if you're collecting alimony.

Divorce aside, if a woman is discriminated against and rejected for a loan largely because she is a woman, she has a serious case against the bank. Only thing is, as we'll see in the same chapter on prejudices, she had better be sure of her case and not be merely angry because she was turned down for solid financial, banking reasons that had nothing to do with her sex.

There are allowable exceptions to the law. If you have a joint credit card with your husband, get divorced, and you each are going to pay your own bills, the department store or whoever issued you the joint card will ask you a special set of questions if you apply for a new one in your own name: How much do you earn yourself? How long have you been employed? Other jobs? Other income?

The law also allows a married woman to open bank accounts and charge accounts in her own name, so that she can develop her own credit profile and standing.

Age is another area of discrimination eliminated by this law. We used to have a policy, common to most banks, that we simply didn't make loans to people sixty-five or over, unless the loan was secured by stocks, bonds, or other property.

We figured that someone at that age was retired, living on Social Security or a pension, and couldn't afford the extra expense of a monthly loan payment, even if he thought he could.

These people have a fixed monthly income, we reasoned, and what happens if inflation hits or they get caught by some unexpected, large expense?

Even if the customer were still working, we assumed he could retire at any time.

Now, we have to consider a loan application from an older citizen on the basis of the usual information he gives us and what we get in our credit checks.

I always found it interesting that even though we used to uniformly discriminate against senior citizens, my banking friends in Florida couldn't be happier with them.

Of course, in a way, they had the cream of the crop.

Largely, these were people who could afford to move there to retire, bringing with them all their acquired wealth, including the big chunk of cash they'd recently picked up from the sale of their home. That cash would normally cover the cost of any new home they wanted to buy, so they didn't try to get large mortgages from the banks. Mostly what they needed were short-term loans to carry them for a while, which was good business for my friends.

Fair Debt Collection Practices Act

While this law affects the way banks go about collecting debts from you, in fact it has much greater impact on collection agencies.

They are the scum who used to call you at midnight, threaten you with loss of your job, your home, maybe even your life, if you didn't pay off the few hundred dollars you owed.

You never owe them directly. They don't lend anything. They are professional punks called in to collect by a supposedly respectable bank or department store or finance company after they have thrown up their respectable hands on your case.

The collection company is hired, and depending on how delinquent your loan is and how difficult it'll be to collect, they will receive 10 percent to 50 percent of whatever they can squeeze out of you.

The law now specifically prohibits a number of their more outrageous practices. The collection people are very careful about this law, partly because they want to push the law as far as they can and partly because they have witnessed huge fines and class action suits.

1. *No more "abuse and harassment."* Which I would think would put them all out of business. They may no longer threaten violence to you and your loved ones unless you pay.

Nor may they use profane language in their chats with you.

Nor may they contact you at "an unusual time or place." No more of those terrifying calls between midnight and four A.M. They may call only between eight A.M. and nine P.M., and no more than twice a week.

Further, collection agencies may not call you at your place of work if you tell them that your employer objects to your handling personal business at work and that they are endangering your job if they continue to make such calls.

Bothering you at work was one of their ways of embarrassing you. I once had a problem with American Express, and one of their people called me at the bank. Now, American Express is one of the most sophisticated and careful of all national creditors when it comes to collecting. Still, you can imagine how I felt, sitting at a big vice-president's desk in the bank, receiving such a call. Who might overhear?

The Amex fellow couldn't have been nicer. He merely wanted to verify, he said, that I was sixty days late. And when I confirmed, alas, his claim, he immediately asked if I had any problem with his calling me at the bank. I said I did and asked him to call me about six-thirty that night at home. In fact, I did not get a call that night, but a few nights later. Meanwhile, no one bothered me at work.

A related prohibition limits the people with whom the collection agency may discuss your case: only with your spouse and, through their lawyer, your lawyer.

They cannot, for example, go to your employer, as they used to enjoy doing, unless you completely disappear on them and they are forced to ask where you might be.

2. *No more "false and misleading representation".* They may not threaten to report false credit information on you to other creditors, or credit bureaus, to instill the fear of total credit annihilation. "When we're through

with you, you won't be able to borrow a dime, charge a
pair of underwear..." They were good at happy, if
false, promises of that sort.

Nor may they use another common ruse, collection
papers made to look like legal documents. Lots of
"heretofores" and "to wits" sprinkled across the legal-
sized sheet, with the accompanying caller telling you on
the phone that they are about to give their attorneys
those same documents to process in court... unless, of
course, you make an immediate payment or settlement.

3. *No more "unfair practices."* A wide range of tricks
are covered here. They may not any longer send you
postcards to inform you of your unpaid debt—and in
the process to inform your mailman, your superintendent,
your neighbors, your family.

Nor may they use the old postdated check trick. This
one worked when you got tired of the chase and you
could also see a bit of light at the end of your personal
tunnel. Your dreadful situation was improving; you were
paying off bills at last, and you could imagine that
before long you'd also be able to pay off the $290 you
still owed Diners.

"Fine," says Charlie from Super Collection of Chicago,
"that's great news. When do you think you'll be able to
pay?"

"Oh, by March," you tell him.

"Okay, tell you what. Because you've been so delinquent on this one, I can't go back and tell them wait till
March. They'll wipe out your credit altogether if I do
that. Tell you what. Can you afford $50 now?"

"Fifty dollars," you reply, disposed to working out a
plan with this helpful fellow, "yes, I guess so."

"Okay, tell you what. You help me, I'll help you.
Send me a check dated today for $50. Send me along
with it another check for $50, dated, say, January 15.
And send a third check, in the same envelope, dated
March 1, and make that for the balance, $190. That
way, you've stretched out the payments, made it easy

on yourself, and you've given me a chance. I can go back and show them the checks, they know the whole thing will be cleared up by March 1."

You send Charlie the three checks, and he deposits them immediately. Nine times out of ten, Charlie knows, a postdated check goes through undetected, especially in the largest banks. He wants his money now.

You have $1,000 in the account to cover rent, phone, and other current bills that you've been struggling madly to pay regularly, so your entire life doesn't collapse. This month, however, you're in for new surprises and troubles. Charlie has hit you for $290.

Today, Charlie could get his company a $5,000 fine for his "unfair practice."

Though these consumer protection laws are taken very seriously by creditors, there are still people who try to beat the law, and there are ways you can defend yourself.

Let me suggest the simplest way of all: Scare them in return.

If you get called by some collector trying some of his old harassment tactics, tell him you know times have changed. "Look, Jack, under the Fair Debt Collection Practices Act, what you're doing is clearly abuse and harassment. Let me talk to your supervisor . . ."

It might sound too simple to be true, but consider a couple of things. First, impressions matter. You are not dealing with a very classy gentleman, when you are talking to a debt collector. If he hears someone speaking good English, telling him about the law—which he knows is there—he is very likely to back off.

Also, I have been told by friends in the credit business that they are all terrified of major lawsuits, especially class action suits, and employees collecting debts have been warned that anybody who sounds like trouble is to be handled with extreme caution.

I had a chance to test it out. I had a foolish fight going with Amoco. I owed them $207—I do recall the exact amount—and wouldn't pay them because they irritated me so. I know that's no way for a banker to behave, but we are also human at times.

Finally, a collection agent called me at seven-thirty on a Saturday morning, woke me up, threatened to take me to court.

"Give me your boss," I screamed at the man. "The law explicitly prohibits you from calling me in my home at seven-thirty on a Saturday morning, and you know it, and I'm going to sue you for harassment."

The guy sputtered and hung up. Months later I got a call from another collection agency. They were almost apologetic. Could they verify a balance I seemed to have with Amoco? Perhaps there was some error, and I didn't actually owe Amoco that amount?

We worked everything out in a few minutes, and I paid my bill.

If you are harassed in any way by a collection agency, as a last resort, you can sue them.

If you're bringing a civil suit, you must start your action within a year of the violation of the law. And if you are going this route, see if it is possible to bring a class action suit. They can be difficult and costly, but they are worth considering if you can assume that you are not alone in your treatment by the collection company and that there are others who will happily join your cause.

There was a major suit in 1980 that stunned the whole credit and collection world. It struck Avco Financial Services, one of the largest loan companies in the state of New York. In 1979, they made some 50,000 loans, amounting to more than $82 million.

Avco was harassing customers who owed them money. They threatened them with physical mutilation and even with death. In their zeal, they made threatening phone calls, not only to the debtors, but to their employers, their friends, their relatives, including a child.

The Bureau of Consumer Frauds and Protection in the Attorney General's Office of the State of New York got complaints about Avco. In July 1979, they had about a dozen and decided they'd check around. They figure that for each complaint like this, normally there are another ten to fifteen damaged parties who are too scared or too embarrassed to go public.

They compared notes with the consumer offices in the Federal Trade Commission and other consumer agencies, and soon they had 200 complaints, and they launched a huge suit against Avco.

They got an injunction from the court that strictly limited the collection practices of Avco. And they made an out-of-court settlement with the company, in which Avco paid court costs of $5,000 and another $85,000 to a fund for the harassed borrowers. One hundred and twenty of the people complaining were paid between $100 and $2,500, depending on the severity of their case.

The results sent sharp signals through the credit and collection world that doing what used to be business as usual was now an extremely costly way of operating.

Checklist:

Establishing credit

1. Open a checking account.
2. Open charge accounts, lots of them. And use them—wisely.
3. Consider making your first loan someplace other than your bank. Talk with your bank officer about the chances and problems of getting your first loan from them before you apply.
4. Consider making that first loan from your company's credit bureau.
5. Find a cosigner.

Checklist:

Protecting your credit

1. If your loan application is rejected, ask your banker if it's because of your credit report.
2. Get that report (if you haven't gotten it already).
3. Correct any errors in it, no matter how tedious the process.
4. Then, go back to your banker for a new shot at the loan.
5. If new trouble hits—like you lose your job and can't pay the loan—tell your banker. Never hide.
6. Understand the Truth in Lending Act: How much the loan is actually going to cost you.
7. Understand the Fair Credit Reporting Act: You can get your own credit report and keep it accurate.
8. Understand the Equal Credit Opportunity Act: No bank may deny you a loan because of your race, age, sex, or marital status.
9. Understand the Fair Debt Collection Practices Act: No more "abuse or harassment" from debt collectors, or "false or misleading" threats from them, or "unfair practices."

Chapter 8

Loans: How to get what you want... what really counts on the loan application

It's time to redo the kitchen. You've been in the house for eight years, and when you bought it, the one serious reservation your wife had was the kitchen. Too cramped, too old, depressing. Your only serious reservation about the house was the fact that it cost much more than you thought you two could afford. Nevertheless, you both bought the place, and you promised her at the time that the next great goal in life was that kitchen. Complete renovation: break through the wall to the pantry, new equipment, a butcher block island, tiled floor, and lights that would finally let you see what you were cooking.

You were sincere in your promise, but life has not permitted you to deliver. Finally, you both decide that the cost of your dream is rising every year and soon will reach what the whole house cost eight years ago. Thanks to that same inflation, it's practically impossible to live decently and save as well. Life's pleasures, however, cannot be deferred forever. "If we're ever going to enjoy that kitchen," your wife points out, "we'd better do it before we're dead."

You give your banker a call, make an appointment, and go in to discuss what you call "our dream plan" and he calls "a consumer loan."

Your bank is not all-knowing, after all

When it comes to consumer loans, the most common all-purpose installment loan, there are some strange laws of banking physics at play. Things are not what you would imagine them to be, and to see clearly at times, you have to use mirrors.

First, there is the whole matter of computers vs. humans.

The greater the loan volume a bank has, the more computerized the whole process is. Yet, your banker can frequently overrule the computer. But he won't do it, he won't become at all involved in your case, unless you motivate him and plug him into the whole process. We'll see how, shortly.

Then, there is the mysterious business of what is supposed to be terribly important in deciding the loan, but which may have no basis in the real world. Let me explain.

Of all the information you provide your bank on a loan application, there are two items that transcend all others: the purpose of your loan and your gross annual income.

On the surface, that would seem to make sense. After all, if you are going to use their $10,000 for something meaningful, like improving your home, or paying medical bills, rather than something frivolous like new clothes and an extended skiing holiday in Switzerland, it stands to reason the loan will mean more to you, its benefits will be lasting, and you will be that much more likely to pay them back their ten grand on time.

Seems to make sense. Only catch is, they have no

way of knowing whether or not you're telling them the truth. You can put down on the application "To pay for triple by-pass open heart surgery" and, instead, have the time of your life on the slopes of Zermatt and Klosters, and they'll never know. And the truth is, just so long as you pay them back as you're supposed to, they don't really care.

Obviously, what you earn in a year should matter greatly. There's no logic or banking sense in lending you $10,000, if all you earn is $25,000 because once you get finished with taxes and your normal living expenses, you won't have enough left to pay off the loan. Simple arithmetic.

Common banking practice in deciding how much to lend you is to figure a percentage of your salary as a safe upper range. The percentage varies according to the prevailing economic climate and the loan policies of particular banks, but these days a normal percentage would be 20 percent. You want $10,000, then show them a salary of $50,000. If all you're earning is $25,000, 20 percent of that is only $5,000, and that's all the formula says you should get.

Only catch here is, it is very unlikely that they really know what you earn. Increasingly, employers are not willing to spend the money it costs to have somebody in personnel look up your records. They might be able to verify a general salary range for a particular job, but even that, if they do it, is only a guess.

Beyond which, an ever increasing number of banks are simply not bothering to verify what you tell them. They too have decided it is not worth their time, that there are other checks and supports they can rely on.

When I share this rather startling piece of intelligence with friends—that banks do not check out what they put down as their salary—they turn larcenous right before my eyes. "You mean I could say I earn $100,000, even if I only earn $35,000, and they'd never know?"

Not exactly. There are human beings reviewing your information, however hastily, at various stages of the

loan process. And if you put an earnings figure down
that is clearly out of line, some kind of check will be
made. In that case, you lie, you lose.

But if you do make $30,000, and put down $35,000,
maybe even $40,000, and for your kind of work that
isn't preposterous, the bank will never know. And they
will still apply their 20 percent ratio, but this time you
will magically qualify for an extra $2,000 in credit.

As startling as some of this might sound, don't think
that your bank is simply flipping a coin when it comes
to deciding whether or not to give you $10,000.

It does have your credit report, and that gives them
quite a full profile of how you've handled your loans
and credit over the last seven to ten years.

It also has its own general loan profiles, and the
statistics show them that only 1.8 percent of all consumer loans go unpaid. That's a workable percentage for
medium to large banks in New York, varying a bit
according to a bank's policies on writing off loans.

What that means to banks is it isn't worth the time
and money to check any more than they do.

The Internal Revenue Service talks of "voluntary
compliance," that people voluntarily pay their taxes and
voluntarily comply with the law. The vast majority of
taxpayers, the IRS has discovered, are honest.

Something of the same thing applies to banks and its
loan customers. The vast majority is honest, put truth-
ful information down on their loan applications, and pay
off their loans.

There is, however, a great difference. The IRS has
various techniques that are designed to keep folks
honest. They audit, for example, sometimes because
they have good reason to think you're cheating, but
sometimes because they want you to spread the word in
your town and among your friends and the people you
work with that they "got" you. It makes all those other
people hesitate before they lie on their returns.

Banks have no such weapons. They operate on what
has proved to be a reasonable business risk, as well as
one deep assumption about you: They know that you

are in fear of losing your credit. Maybe you will fudge your statistics, get a little creative when you fill out your loan application. But in the end, you know the limits of the game. You must pay them back. Because if you don't, you can be absolutely certain that the news of your default will appear prominently on your credit report, and you will be out of the personal loan business for many years to come.

With that fresh, insider's perspective, let's now consider the four most important elements that affect the bank's decision to give you a loan, or not.

1. *The credit scoring system*. The bank wants you to be "stable." If you own your own home and have lived there for more than five years, they give you points for that, many more than they would give you if you rented and bounced around all the time. Same with your job. The longer you're there, the better, the more points. There are other indices for scoring, as we'll see.

Get 150 points on a 200-point system, and you get the loan, other things being equal. Under 80, quick rejection. Between 100 and 140, you're in the gray zone, which is when and where you need your banker to intervene.

Not all banks use these point-scoring systems. Smaller ones still tend to have their bank officers make their own evaluations and recommendations. But again, volume usually decides. One exception is CIT, the huge finance company. They make tens of thousands of loans a year, and they don't use any point system. Don't believe in it. They think the judgment of their loan officer, after he has had a chance to meet and talk with you, together with your credit report are enough to go on.

2. *Your credit report*. Given what I've told you about how little banks verify of your data, it should be no surprise that between 50 percent to 70 percent of the

bank's decision will depend on what the credit service reports to them.

When we examine the actual loan-processing system, we'll see how important it is that you forewarn your banker of any dreadful news that might be waiting in your credit report.

3. *The 20 percent–25 percent ratio*. In theory, this will keep you from going so heavily in debt you won't be able to pay them back.

So, they figure it's safe to lend you up to 20 percent of your annual income.

Or, they apply another ratio that relates to the amount of debt you are already carrying. They take the amount of the loan you're after, add it to the outstanding debts you list on the loan application, and that total should not come to more than 25 percent of your annual gross earnings.

You want them to lend you $10,000 and you show current debts to American Express, Sears, Exxon, and Gump's department store, which come to, say, $3,000? The bank would perceive you theoretically in debt for $13,000, if they make the loan to you. They do not want that amount to be greater than 25 percent of your income, which means in this case you should show them at least $52,000.

Actually, they would prefer that the loan brings you to less than 25 percent because they figure that you'll probably borrow or charge more, before your loan to them is paid off, and so have additional debt to manage. They'd like a cushion.

4. *Your relationship with your banker.* In the end, it can all come back to this. Despite the numbers you show, what does he think the bank can trust you to pay back? But he won't make that decision, or put himself on the line for you, unless you motivate him. Otherwise, chances are, your banker will do little more than process your application. He or she sits at the center of the

whole system, but their natural instinct is to deal with your loan application as automatically as the scoring computer. You can change that, as we'll see, and it can make the difference between getting the loan and going away empty-handed.

Let's examine the whole loan process, observing how and when each of these elements comes into play along the way.

It starts with your filling out the "Installment Loan Application Form." I've included a sample here from The Bank of New York. It's typical, and if we go through it line by line, as I've numbered them, you'll see how the point-scoring system works and the bank sketches out your financial profile.

1. Charge my checking account for payments

This matters. You get points, if you let the bank take the monthly payments automatically from your checking account. It's not a major consideration. But the bank would rather not depend on your remembering to come in and pay at the beginning of each month, never mind have to worry that you won't pay, or juggle your payment along with five others when you hit a tight stretch.

2. Send mail to

A convenience for the customer. If you have your loan correspondence sent to your office, your bank officer assumes you don't want your husband or wife to know about the loan. Doesn't mean anything, unless you're a borderline case and your bank officer has to ask you a lot of questions.

3. Purpose of loan

In theory, as I said, this is extremely important. "A good purpose makes a good loan" I was told over and over, and as we saw, there's a certain amount of logic to that.

You want $10,000 to improve your home. One of the

INSTALMENT LOAN APPLICATION FORM PLEASE PRINT CLEARLY.

AMOUNT OF LOAN APPLIED FOR (please print)

Specify Amount (Minimum $1000)

1 □ Credit my checking account for proceeds □ yes □ no
□ Charge my checking account for payments □ yes □ no
Bank of New York Checking Account Name
Bank of New York Checking Account #
2 Send mail to □ Home □ Business

3 PURPOSE OF LOAN (please print)

Specify

4 PERSONAL (please print)

5 EMPLOYMENT (please print)

9 OTHER INCOME (please print)

10 REPAYMENT PERIOD (please print)

Number of months

11 BANK ACCOUNTS (please print)

12 FINANCIAL OBLIGATIONS (please print)

13

14

SIGNATURE(S) Each party who will be contractually liable for the loan must sign below

15 JOINT APPLICATION (please print)

16 INSURANCE (please print)

17

18

19

20

THE BANK OF NEW YORK

best reasons you could have. At once, you're increasing the value of your home, and you're inproving the way you live.

Paying off your medical bills, or taxes, or consolidating all your bills into one and spreading out the time you'll have to pay them off—all good reasons. Each of those will seriously affect your life, and the bank knows that will make you all the more motivated to pay back on time.

If the loan is for less serious matters, like a vacation, the pleasure goes quickly, and the loan payments linger.

In fact, however, the bank doesn't know whether you're telling them the truth about the purpose of your loan or not. There's no way, with most loans, they can check, and they don't try.

In one way, the bank doesn't much care, so long as the loan is repaid according to terms.

There are exceptions. It really wants to know the truth with car loans and debt consolidation loans. For cars, the bank is going to own the car with you, take title to the car with you, and keep it until the loan is paid off.

On loans where you want to consolidate your debts, the bank will often send its checks directly to the department store and American Express and the furniture store and Exxon, just to be absolutely certain that that's where the money goes. The bank knows that people who get overextended have a way of getting deeper in debt, if they have the temptation. To dramatize the problem, your banker might take all your credit cards when he gives you the loan and, right before your eyes, cut them up.

The bank would really like to know if you're going to take their money and invest it in the stock market, not only because that can be a very risky use of their money but also because the federal government requires the bank to report such loans.

But, once again, if you lie to them, there's nothing they can do. However, when you take their $5,000 and blow it on pork belly futures, don't expect any sympathy. You still have to pay off that loan.

When it comes to large corporate loans, or small business loans, the situation is different. The bank analyzes your company and knows sometimes better than you what your needs are for fresh capital. The bank officer and his evaluation of your business and you and your associates who run the operation play a far greater role from the start than any computer's scoring system.

With your personal loan, however, the bank officer only becomes involved to the degree you make him involved. When that happens, he'll question you about your real plans for the money.

He'll sense if you're lying. He'll also see, just how essential or flimsy your purpose is. Maybe you and your wife really do need a vacation. Two years has been too long, and they've been tough years, and the strains are showing in your health, your marriage, your work. I've given loans for just such reasons, when the customer, whom I knew of course, really opened up to me.

So be prepared. If you plug your banker into your loan process, as you should, and you end up in a gray area—not enough points, say, for a loan as large as you want—and you need your banker's personal intervention, the true purpose you have in mind for that money is going to be extremely significant.

4. Personal

Here's where the bank starts using its scoring system to measure your "stability."

The scoring system is either devised inside the bank, or if the volume of loan applications is great enough, it is a plan the bank buys from one of the outside firms who designs them.

Typically, the firm comes into the bank and studies the bank's recent loan history. Have people who live in one residence over a period of years been paying their loans off more reliably than folks who move around?

How many years seem to matter when it comes to employment?

It also examines the bank's market area and general loan policies. How tight does the bank want to be with its money?

The scoring system, then, becomes a reflection of the bank's lending policies and what the bank considers risky.

They ask you if you own your own home. That's important, because general experience has shown that anyone owning for more than five years is a better risk than someone who rents.

Not only does the statistical evidence lean that way, but the bank also knows that if you own your own home and things get rough, you can't simply say, "The hell with them all..." and move out to Idaho to start all over again, unencumbered by all your debts, including the one you have from the bank.

The bank will not check out the number of years you tell them you've owned your home, nor how long you lived at your previous address. But they'll give you high points for anything more than five years there.

There is one item in the "Personal" category your bank will check, and it is a bit surprising to most people: your home phone number.

First, they want to be sure they can reach you, if trouble comes up. Further, if the phone company has given you a phone, you either have sufficient credit for them to trust you, or you have produced a substantial deposit. Either one is reassuring to the bank.

One question in the "Personal" section gives the bank a hint of marital status: "Number of Dependents." As you can imagine, the bank would like you to show two or three dependents. Too many, and they'll worry about how you can feed all those mouths and pay them back too.

So you will get points for the right answers, but don't get too worried. Just because you are single and renting an apartment, your third in three years, doesn't mean it's a waste of time for you to even fill out an application.

The point totals are only part of the decision process. And even if you score low on some lines, other categories can overwhelm all the other data. Show a salary of $60,000 a year, and your bank quickly shreds its whole costly scoring system.

5. Employment

To be "self-employed" is practically criminal, so far as your bank is concerned.

Self-employed people are here today, out of business tomorrow, the bank says. No stability, when it comes to paychecks. Feast or famine is their normal state.

Anticipate all their anxieties. If you're self-employed and want a loan, go to your appointment with your banker with income tax returns from the last two or three years in hand. Let him see exactly what you've been earning. Maybe he should look at more than two or three years if one of those years was bad.

If you have contracts or letters of agreement for new business, bring those along as well.

By doing that, you'll give him the ammunition he needs to get you the loan, and you'll give him confidence in you. He'll be impressed at your businesslike ways: Even before he asked, you knew to bring in the supporting evidence.

If you have an employer and fill in the name of your company, the bank will call to be sure that you do have a job where you say you do.

6. Position

May or may not be checked, when they call to verify your place of employment. Still, make yourself sound as important as possible. If you work for a sizable corporation, there are people in your personnel department who are paid to come up with fancy-sounding titles for your job. Find out what your official title really is.

I have seen typists become associate administrative assistants. A janitor became an apprentice maintenance engineer. Salespeople are sales executives, or sales managers. All secretaries become administrative secretaries, and of course anyone who is an executive secretary as we've seen, has a perfectly terrific title just as it is.

Any truly managerial title is good because a banker can relate to that. He knows that it takes a long time to rise in an organization, that you have to suffer abuse and be patient, all of which adds to your stability in his eyes.

7. Years There

Very important for your stability score.

Anything more than five to seven years is rated very high. Up to that point, you haven't had any great disappointments yet, the scorers figure, probably haven't had a chance for personal problems to get in the way of work and progress.

Bouncing around among three different jobs over three or four years is suspect. If there are special reasons for your changes, attach a memo to your application and explain. I had a woman applicant who was an independent contractor with various garment firms on Seventh Avenue. She was employed by each company for the length of a particular job, then she moved on to the next. She wasn't technically self-employed, but her record for steadiness didn't look good. I had her attach a note explaining briefly the nature of her business, so some credit reviewer wouldn't automatically penalize her.

8. Your Annual Gross Earnings

Not much more I can tell you here. As critically important as this data obviously is, the practice with the great majority of urban banks is to take your word for what you write in. Smaller banks, rural banks still are likely to call and try to verify your income. But, even they have difficulties. Many companies don't want to bother digging out the accurate information.

One thing to bear in mind, before you declare yourself one of America's highest-paid executives. If anything I've said in this book matters, it is the advice to develop a personal relationship with your banker. It is the real key to getting service from your bank, to getting loans from it as well. Obviously, part of that relationship is honesty. He or she has to know, at some point, what you really are earning, what you really are worth.

I have had customers inflate their income figures on loan applications. When I questioned them, they muttered something about including bonuses and profit-sharing plans. It was clear to me what they were doing, but the truth is, I didn't care. Their distortion was slight. What I was considering was their whole profile, including all the experience I had known with them for some years.

As we follow your pursuit of the $10,000 loan to create a livable kitchen, let's assume you're earning $32,000 a year, and your wife, who's going after this with you, earns $13,000.

Together you show $45,000. If we apply the 20 percent ratio, your loan should be no more than $9,000. Still, as we'll see, all is not lost.

9. Other Income

Usually, what you enter here isn't going to make much difference. Many people think they're strengthening their case by claiming $5,000 additional income from "investments," but they are only kidding themselves. Doesn't mean a thing.

If, in fact, you don't show enough earned income to qualify for a loan, but you show quite a bit of "other income," your banker will ask you for proof. Let me see those stocks and bonds, please. He might even suggest that instead of an installment consumer loan, you should consider a secured loan, where your stocks would be handed over to the bank as collateral.

But remember, even there, he's got to believe that one way or another you'll have the income to pay off the interest, and the loan itself, when it comes due. Those securities in the bank's vault only give them some insurance and protection. They never want to have to sell those off in order to cover your loan.

One of the trickiest items in the "other income" category is alimony.

As we saw, federal law, often buttressed by state law, now prohibits banks from asking you if you're married. One of the points of The Equal Credit Opportunity Act is to prevent discrimination against someone, simply because he or she is not married.

Still, the banks would like to know because prejudices die hard, and in their minds, there is no question, a married person, male or female, is a better risk than a swinging single.

Because these laws are seriously applied and fines are attached for violations, a banker today is going to be extremely careful about asking any question that might in any way suggest that he's coyly trying to skirt the law. Every consumer loan application in the country will carry on it, near the section where it inquires about "Other Income," a statement along these lines: "Income from alimony, child support, or maintenance payments need not be revealed if the Applicant does not choose to disclose such income in applying for credit."

Precisely because of that widespread prejudice, I think it's wisest not to note anything about alimony or the rest.

However, if you really don't think your earned income is going to be sufficient to get you the loan, add your alimony. The bank is required to consider it as additional income.

Another disclosure dilemma for many when they come to "Other Income" concerns their second jobs. Very common today are second jobs that are "off the books," or where people are paid in cash. They don't declare that income on their tax returns, and they are wary of letting the bank know for fear the IRS will somehow get access to the information.

Their fears are well founded. Banks make efforts to protect information, but the efforts vary. They won't tell anything they're not supposed to if some business competitor of yours calls up trying to find out more about you. But the IRS has its ways. They are supposed to obtain court orders if they want to study your bank accounts. But often they don't bother, and the branch manager simply decides to cooperate with the intimidating fellows with the badges in their pockets.

Nevertheless, there are times when you have to take a chance. I had one applicant who was a bartender. He needed $5,000 to buy into a bar, and his salary of about $10,000 didn't come close to justifying a loan of that size.

But I knew the fellow. He worked in my old neighborhood, and I had been his bank officer for some years. There was no doubt in my mind that he'd pay back any amount we lent him.

After reviewing the whole thing with him, I told him that the only chance he had for the loan would be to give us his true income.

He winced. "Tips, everything?"

"Tips, everything."

"I hate to do that, John."

"I understand, but I don't see any choice. Not if you want the loan," I told him. "Ever have any trouble with the IRS?"

"Not yet," he replied.

He decided to take a chance. In addition to his $10,000 salary, he pocketed about $20,000 more, off the books, cash. This was some time ago, and $30,000 was much more than I or practically anybody else on the floor of the bank was earning at the time.

It wasn't easy, but by lobbying very hard for the fellow, I got him his $5,000 loan. He bought into his bar, never missed a payment, paid the loan back, and to the best of my knowledge never got audited by the IRS.

10. Repayment Period
Lots of people think they'll improve their chances for the loan if they say they'll pay it back quickly.

The bank doesn't care about that. What the bank

wants is a repayment schedule you can live with. In
fact, when the bank evaluates your ability to repay, the
time you take is a factor. Often loans are made on the
condition that a longer repayment schedule is part of
the deal.

So far as they're concerned, their money is earning
interest. They don't stretch loans out just to increase
their profits. The sooner they have your loan money
back, the sooner they can lend it elsewhere. They
stretch loans out because they don't want you collapsing
on them, strapping yourself to the point where you
can't make payments.

You have up to forty-eight months on most consumer
loans, so make yourself a schedule that is comfortable.
You won't lose points here.

One exception is loans for taxes. An awful lot of
people don't withhold enough or put aside enough to
make their tax payments, not only this year but every
year. The bank doesn't want to support that habit.

You need a loan for taxes and have proof, fine, a very
good reason to borrow. But let us have the money back
in nine months to a year. That way, you won't still be
owing us, if you hit more of the same kind of trouble
next year.

11. Bank Accounts

Get yourself a savings account. It looks good, and
even though it is highly unlikely that the bank will ever
check your balance, it gets you points.

If you anticipate now that in six months you'll need a
bank loan, go and open a savings account today.

Often, of course, you can't get a loan from a bank
unless you have a checking account with them, and
unless your bank officer is buried in work, he'll verify
your average balance. For this $10,000 home loan you're
after, an average balance of about $800 will look good.
As I noted earlier, a Regular Checking Account confers
much higher status on you than a Special Checking
Account.

12. Financial Obligations

We saw how the bank will add up all the debts you list here, combine that figure with the amount of the loan you're after, and be sure that the total of new indebtedness doesn't exceed 25 percent of your annual income.

They do not include the amount of your monthly mortgage payments or your car payments. Those figures would distort the ratio too much.

But they will look closely at all your other financial obligations and check them against your credit report. Be extremely careful here. There is a special warning on this application. "NOTE: Failure to list all debts will disqualify this request."

They mean it. If you think you'll be clever and conveniently forget about a debt or two, you're going to have your loan application rejected out of hand.

Extremely important are any other bank loans you have, or applications for loans.

Banks in the main money centers used to have their own central file for this information. In New York, it was called Group Interchange, and every bank reported every loan application daily to The New York Clearing House, the place where checks written on the various banks in the New York area are tabulated and exchanged.

Today, with the swiftness of computers and the thoroughness of credit companies, all that data goes through the credit bureaus.

As soon as you apply at one bank for a loan, that information is flashed to TRW, or whatever credit company the bank uses. If you stroll into another bank half-an-hour later and file a second application, that bank will not only inform their credit company, but when they pull a credit report on you, they will discover that only minutes before, the ink hardly dry on the application, you went after loan number one.

There is nothing at all wrong with your having a loan with one bank and asking for another from a different bank. All the second bank cares about is how much you still owe their competitor and how you've been paying them off.

But if you hide one loan application, or bank loan, and go after another, it will show up in one of your credit reports, and you will receive an automatic rejection.

If you've borrowed a thousand dollars from your brother-in-law, that's between the two of you. But be sure to list anything other than a personal loan like that.

13. Comaker or Guarantor

Someone you work with asks you to cosign a loan for him. He explains how easy it'll be for him to pay it back, how you'll have no worries. Be careful.

First of all, there is a reason the bank has told your colleague to get someone else's signature on the loan along with his own. He doesn't have enough credit to qualify for the loan himself.

When I was a junior officer at the bank, I had a fellow in my department ask me to cosign for $6,000. He was overextended a bit, he explained, but he was taking care of that. Until he did, however, like everyone else, he couldn't borrow.

I didn't like to say no, so I hedged, told him I already had plenty of debts myself, which I did, and anything like that, I had to discuss with my wife.

She was against it, for the very good reason that it didn't feel right to her.

I told him the next day that she was nervous about getting involved in any additional debts at this time. He shrugged, tried to tell me that it really wasn't my debt. I shrugged, and that was that.

Six weeks later, my fellow junior officer vanished. A long time later, he surfaced in Nashville. Bank officer or not, he was so overextended, flight was the only solution he could come up with.

If I had cosigned on that loan, I would have owed the bank $6,000, despite what he said. To any bank making a loan with cosigners, both people are equally responsible for repaying the loan.

Countless people don't understand that. They are

simply being friendly, they think. In fact, they are assuming the liability of their friend's loan.

Most people also don't understand that if they have cosigned for a loan, it will be considered a "financial obligation" when they go to apply for a loan of their own. Their bank will look at it just as they look at the amount of, say, credit card debts being carried. And the more existing "financial obligation" you have, the less the bank will want to lend you.

I advise people never to cosign, unless it's for someone very near and dear. A relative in trouble is tough to turn away. But otherwise, be friendly but don't sign.

If you have cosigned, be certain to tell your banker the exact state of that loan. If it is being handled properly, you will still be considered holding a debt, but you won't receive any marks for late payment, or worse.

14. Judgments, Bankruptcies, etc.

These are the worst credit black marks you can show, and if you have any, be sure to tell all. The bank will pick these up routinely from their credit bureau, and if you tried to hide anything, they will reject your loan application.

If you had any such trouble, and it's been cleared up, it is essential that you discuss everything with your banker, and probably attach a memo as well.

15. Joint Application

The obvious benefit of going for a loan with someone else, almost always a spouse, is the addition of a second income to bolster your case. Here, we are assuming she has $13,000 to add to your $32,000. Understanding the 20 percent formula, you can see how significant that additional income can be.

The bank, by the way, will consider the person with the higher income, the primary applicant. And they will place greater emphasis on that person's credit report.

Both parties are equally responsible, and if there is

trouble, the bank will come after both. This gets sticky if the loan outlives the marriage, which is not uncommon. It's a problem banks dread, but even so, applying jointly will not cost you points. What the bank is interested in is the total joint income working to pay off their loan.

16. Insurance

On this application, you have a choice of life insurance, or life and accident and health. A typical arrangement.

It has no effect on the scoring, but I recommend that you take both. The premiums are low, with the life premium diminishing as the loan gets paid off.

If you die without the insurance, your estate would be liable for the balance of the loan, which could be a burden on the estate and so, your heirs.

With the accident and health coverage, if you are incapacitated and can't pay off the loan, the insurance does it for you.

17. "To Obtain or Exchange . . . Information"

Here in the small print, which most people never read, you are giving the bank the right to exchange information about you with your employer, the creditors, anyone they think they need to consult, in order to decide what to do with your application.

18. "True Answers"

In this sentence, not only are you affirming that everything you've told them on the application is true, but if they decide to base their loan decision on nothing but what you've told them, that's all they ever need. If you later go broke, you have no defense if you turn around and say to them: "Well, I made a mistake. I forgot about that other $10,000 I owed. And, I guess I exaggerated my earnings a bit. But you should have checked out what I told you in the first place."

No defense at all. They can still come after you for the loan and sue you for fraud.

19. Material Changes

If you move, this sentence says, you've got to tell the bank. No hiding behind the excuse that you didn't get the monthly loan bill in the mail because they mailed it to your old address.

Similarly, if there are any other important changes in your life that affect the information on the application, you have to tell them.

They especially want to hear from you, and early, if you go bankrupt.

20. Credit Report

This gives the bank your permission to pull a complete credit report on you.

It also gives you, as noted earlier, the right to find out from them where they got the report. Remember, they do not have to and won't give you the report. But they are required under the Fair Credit Reporting Act to tell you, if you ask, exactly which credit bureau they used, and that credit bureau is required to give you a copy of the same report.

Checklist:

The four most important elements in your bank's loan decision

1. The credit scoring system.
2. Your credit report.
3. The 20 percent–25 percent ratio.
4. Your relationship with your banker.

Checklist:

What matters most on your loan application

1. *Purpose of the loan.* Home improvement, medical bills, paying of taxes, coordinating all your bills into one—all needs the bank highly respects.

2. *Personal "stability."* Scoring system gives you high points for things like living in your own home more than five years, and holding the same job more than five to seven years.

3. *Annual gross earnings.* Basically the bank wants to keep your loan to 20 percent of what you make— or what you and your joint applicant together make if you have someone applying for the loan with you.

4. *Your other existing financial obligations.* The bank will add them up and combine that with the amount of the loan you're after to keep the total of your new indebtedness to 25 percent of your annual income. Otherwise, they fear you won't be able to handle it all.

Chapter 9

More on loans: Plugging in your banker... The critical difference

Now is the time to activate your bank officer. Up to this point in the loan process, he has merely responded mechanically. You called him, told him you wanted to come in and apply for a loan. Fine, he said, and you set a time. When you arrived, he gave you the loan application, and you filled in all the blanks.

Now do not just hand it to him and leave, praying. Engage him in a conversation about it. Brief as it might be, it is terribly important.

Otherwise, all he's going to do is attach a form that records the date, your name, the amount you want, and put it in his out box. He could be busy, or he could be indifferent. Amounts to the same thing for you.

If he simply passes the application along for processing, your case will not receive any personal attention. From here on out, even though human beings will be reviewing your information, the whole process will be predetermined and mechanical.

First, review the amount you want with him.

Bearing in mind the 20 percent–25 percent ratio, ask him if you're going after too big a loan. We are considering a $10,000 loan, where there is a combined gross income for you and your wife of $45,000. Let's assume you and your wife are also showing debts of $3,000.

Looking at the application, he can see the disparity. By strict interpretation of the rules, on your $45,000 income, he should lend you 20 percent, or $9,000.

He can also see that if he gives you the $10,000 you're after and adds the $3,000 debt to that, you'll be in debt for $13,000. Doing the rest of his arithmetic, and calculating 25 percent of your income, he comes up with $11,250, as the maximum debt you two should be carrying, if everyone wants to be completely safe.

Let him maneuver...

But maybe, he's not so concerned about that theoretical $1,800 that is over his limit. Maybe, furthermore, as you review the matter with him, you can tell him about a new promotion that's coming, about a new contract you've landed. And maybe, you're talking to him at a time when the bank has decided to make more consumer loans. There's a new marketing policy, which you know nothing about, but it calls for the bank to get more aggressive in the area of consumer loans, and you're going to be one of the first beneficiaries.

However, it's also possible that money is tight, so your banker will begin to ask you about doing with less. "If we could get only $9,000 for you, could you live with that? Maybe use Mexican tile on that new kitchen floor, instead of those beautiful French things?..."

He's anticipating a call from the credit reviewer. "This guy's asking for too much, Dave. His TRW isn't bad, and he scores okay, but the income isn't there. And with the debts they already have, we give them $10,000, they're going to be awfully strapped meeting all those payments."

"Supposing we made it for $9,000?"

"At $9,000, we could justify that up here, Dave, no problem."

That's the exchange he wants to be able to have, if the call comes. He might tell you that it's worth trying for the full $10,000, especially if you give him the fallback position of $9,000.

. . . fully armed

This is also the time to tell Dave about any bad news his credit reviewers might encounter. Prepare him to defend you. You can be certain that the huge fight you had four years ago with Macy's, for example, is fully documented on your credit report. Flag it, and explain exactly what happened. How they kept sending your bills to your old address, even though you had notified them of your new address, and the further confusion of your paying off one amount to them and thinking the whole thing was covered, especially when you never got another bill. And then the whole saga about clearing it up once and for all with their collection lawyers.

If you've had nightmare experiences like that—and who hasn't?—bring along whatever papers you have to document your case. Your banker may do no more than flip through them, just to be sure they're the real thing, but he'll be impressed with your careful manner.

An awful lot of people are afraid or ashamed of the credit problems they've had and say nothing, hoping, I suppose, that the bank somehow won't find out. But they make a dreadful mistake. The bank does find out, and rather than arming their banker with the full story, they leave him open to surprise attack. It might come in another, different kind of call from the credit reviewer.

These days especially, bankers know that credit problems are as common as colds, and everybody catches them. Do not be ashamed or try to hide that sad personal history. You could lose yourself a loan.

Get your credit report before he does

In fact, allow me to repeat a bold piece of advice: Before you go for your loan, it's a good idea to get your credit report and look it over. Even if you think your past is clean, there might be troubles you have blanked out, or there might be erroneous information against you.

Call your banker, ask him which credit agency they use. Call them and get it. They'll charge a small fee about $10. (You only get it free if you've been turned down for a loan or other credit due to information in the report.)

Do not go in for your loan meeting waving the report. Do not ask your banker to review it with you and advise you on how it shapes up. Remember, you have a good business relationship with him, but he still works for the bank. He still has to maintain some dispassionate judgment on your case, even when he wants to help you.

But whatever you find in the report that might cause trouble, you can certainly tell him about, arming him with your side of the story, documented if possible.

Not all the news you give your banker in this chat must be dismal. Give him success stories and also remind him a bit of your good banking record. He might not have time to check, or even remember you all that well, so tell him that you've been keeping good average balances in your accounts, and that you've been a customer of the bank for three years, five years, whatever it's been.

Your entire discussion with your banker may take no more than ten or fifteen minutes. But you have immeasurably improved your loan chances.

A few words from him can matter

When you leave his desk, your banker will fill out an internal transmittal form and attach it to your application.

As you can see, looking at the form from The Bank of New York, much of this sheet covers the rudimentary information the bank needs to log your loan application.

But there is also space for your banker's comments. He is not required to write a word in there. However, if your short conversation with him was effective, he will, and his words can affect the whole loan process.

The first important lines for you come in the "Depositor Experience" section.

Actually, much of the historical information on your accounts, he might write down as you told him. He might have seven to ten applications to handle that day, along with his other work, and not have time to check out your records. So he takes your word for that information.

But if he does check, or he recalls unpleasant experiences with you and bounced checks, he will place an X in that "Returned Checks" box, and you have a serious black mark against you.

Under "Related Accounts" he might note that your company also does business with the bank or that other members of your family do. All this related business is important. The credit department is alerted by such a comment that this is not just another loan application.

What he says in the next category, "Recommendation By Interviewer," can make or break you.

If he checks the "decline" box, forget it. You are not going to get your new kitchen through his bank. Checking "approval" obviously helps, but it does not automatically mean you get the loan you want.

If he leaves the "Comments" section empty, it signals the credit department that he doesn't know you and/or doesn't care about you and your business. In that case, everything will be decided by the numbers you show, an automatic process.

▦ THE BANK OF NEW YORK

APPLICATION TRANSMITTAL AND REGISTER

Date:_____

To: **CONSUMER CREDIT DEPARTMENT**

From: _____
Name of Banking Office   Extension #   Region

Applicant _____

Type of Loan: ☐ Conv. Credit   ☐ Exec. Credit
☐ Instalment   ☐ Master Charge

Amount $_____ Term_____ Rate_____   ☐ LESS Payout of LOAN #_____

☐ PLUS Payout of LOAN #_____

Form checked (x) attached hereto:

☐ Application   ☐ Comaker's Statement   ☐ Insurance Form   ☐ Accident & Health Form
☐ Note   ☐ Security Agreement   ☐ Contractors Estimate   ☐ Other _____

DEPOSITOR EXPERIENCE

Account Since	Type of Account	Number	Title of Account			Returned Checks	
						OD	UN
_____	☐ Savings _____		_____	Pres. Bal.			
_____	☐ Sp. Ck. _____		_____	Aver. Bal.			
_____	☐ Reg. Ck. _____		_____	Aver. Bal.			

Related Accounts _____

Commercial Borrowing: _____

RECOMMENDATION BY INTERVIEWER:

APPROVAL ☐   URBAN AFFAIRS LOAN: YES ☐ NO ☐

DECLINE ☐   (If yes complete reverse side)

Comments: _____

_____

_____

Interviewer _____

DISPOSITION OF LOAN:

Branch Office Approval ☐

Branch Office Approval ☐ (Subject to Credit Check)

Branch to Issue ☐   Account Credited #_____

CCD to Issue   ☐   Check Issued   #_____

Approved By _____   Approval # _____

CONSUMER CREDIT DEPT. RESPONSE:	BANKING OFFICE NOTIFICATION OF ACTION TAKEN:
Date Received _____ By _____	Approval ☐
Comments: _____	Decline ☐
_____	Alternate Offer ☐ _____
_____	
_____	Notified By _____ Date: _____
_____	Customer's
_____	Address _____
_____	_____
	Phone # _____

1-270-0119 (8-77)

Or, he might want to put himself on record, not to help you but to protect himself, in case anything goes wrong with this loan. So, he'd write something like, "Absolutely no special privilege or consideration here . . ." "Treat like a new customer . . ." "Proceed strictly according to current policy and procedures . . ." Once again, the credit department is on notice: He doesn't know and/or care about you and does not feel he can make any special judgment on your application, up or down.

The world is very different, however, if he writes in there: "Applicant is well known to me for three or four years, sound character, steady income, long-term good prospect for various services of the bank . . ." With a statement like that, the credit department will lean toward giving you the loan, and if they have any question about it, they will call your banker and discuss it. They will never mechanically reject you, as they might another loan application with the same numbers, but no supportive comment. They will give your banker a chance to defend you.

There is one further place where your banker can support your case, in the next section, "Disposition of Loan." There is a box, "Branch Office Approval," which the branch manager can check. My own experience has been that it is very rare indeed for a branch manager to want to stick his neck out on a consumer loan like this.

At this point, your banker is finished with the application, for now. He puts it in his out box, and it will be taken to the Credit Scoring Department, where you will get your points.

How they "score" you

As we saw, when it comes to scoring, what the bank is trying to measure, quickly, is your "stability" and your ability to pay the loan back.

Your application goes to a clerk who sits with the

bank's current scorecard on one side and a computer terminal on the other.

Depending on the scoring system the bank is using, he will quickly pick out the ten or so pieces of information to be graded.

"Okay, let's see, this guy owns own home, good for twenty points... Has owned for six years, very good, another twenty points... Years in job come to nine, which is terrific, for thirty points..."

Each line and the points awarded are punched into the computer and added up.

He then refers to the latest guidelines from the bank's Consumer Credit Policy Committee. Once a scoring system is installed, a bank has to adjust it every quarter or so to keep it consistent with its changing loan policies. They shift all the time, depending on the economy and how tight money is, how aggressive a bank wants to be in the business of going after loans, any number of reasons. The scoring has to be adjusted accordingly. Otherwise, at a time when the bank wants to make more loans, it could find itself losing a lot of business, a lot of loans being rejected because of the arbitrary point count.

The scoring clerk knows nothing about policy, and he has no authority to make any decisions. His job is to read your numbers, attach weighted values to them, and then check your totals against the guidelines from on high. This month, they read like this for his 200-point system:

0–80: Reject, don't read or review.

80–100: Probable rejection, review carefully, check with loan officer.

100–140: Typical consumer, reasonable risk, review with disposition toward approval.

140–175: Grant the loan, unless there are outstanding contrary reasons.

175–200: Issue loan, refer to marketing.

One of the purposes of these categories is to speed up the whole process. In the lowest category the orders are clear. Don't waste anybody's time with this. Send it right back to the loan officer. Don't bother with a credit check, credit review, nothing.

At the other extreme, the score is so high that there is no question about granting the loan, assuming the credit check doesn't turn up a history of bankruptcies or the like. No need for the credit reviewers to spend much time on this one, only the most cursory scan. Further, the marketing department should be informed that such a healthy customer exists in our bank. Perhaps he would like the bank to manage some of his assets, set up a trust for him, be the executor of his will, who knows what else?

Most people land in one of the three middle categories, requiring a full loan review process.

In your case, let's assume you score a respectable 135 points. Typical consumer, reasonable risk, and other things being equal, they want to give you the loan.

The clerk drops his scorecard into the manila folder that now contains your loan application and the internal transmittal sheet with your banker's comments on it.

Also to be slipped in there by another clerk is the verification of your employer and your home phone number. While you were being scored, he was making his phone calls.

Once that is done, the folder and your case are ready for the credit department.

In the hands of Jerry, the credit reviewer

The credit operations centers of most urban banks are typically located in nearby suburbs. At The Bank of New York, ours used to be in White Plains; now it is in

Harrison, New York. Trucks shuttle among our city branches, fetching and carrying the loan files out there.

At the operations center in Harrison, they are sorted according to type of loan. Yours goes into the Installment pile. Others to Convenience Credit, Executive Credit, or American Express Gold Card, and MasterCard-Visa.

There's a group head for each loan category, three or four credit reviewers under each. The group supervisors divide the work among their credit reviewers.

As we'll see, Jerry, your credit reviewer, has limited power and room for discretion. Essentially, he is there to make judgments the computer is incapable of making. What he decides can give you, through your banker, the chance to explain some questionable credit report, or the chance to argue for more money than a strict interpretation of the guidelines would allow you.

So Jerry matters to you, but even so, in the ladder of the bank, he is only a high-level clerk, with three or four years at his job. When I had loans rejected and wanted to resuscitate them, I wouldn't call Jerry but his boss's boss, the supervisor of the whole credit checking operation.

When Jerry receives your folder along with ten or fifteen others, he does a quick scan. Is all the information there, have you filled in everything? If anything's missing, he'll call Dave, your bank officer, tell him what's needed, and the whole process gets put on hold, until you provide what's needed.

If it's all there, he hands your folder to a computer operator, who logs it in for the bank's records, and then contacts the credit bureau.

Harrison does not connect directly with Anaheim but bounces off the TRW line in New Jersey. The teleprinter flashes your vital statistics, and seven seconds later the Anaheim computer starts typing out your red, white, and blue credit report on the Harrison teleprinter.

Jerry takes it along with your folder and now starts reviewing seriously.

First, he applies the 20 percent–25 percent ratio

standards. Often he finds cases where the income levels
lift an applicant way over the ratios. He likes those,
they can be processed quickly. A fast scan of the TRW
report, a check of the points scored, and he's done. He
stamps a big fat "APPROVED" in the box down at the
bottom of the transmittal form, and it goes flying back
to the loan officer. Jerry himself gets points of a sort
from his boss for speed. He might flip through his pile
of applications, to see if there are any other people with
heavy incomes to whip through in a flash.

With others, like you, more time is needed on
everything. He takes note that you and your wife show
$45,000 joint income, with outstanding debts of $3,000.
"Guy wants $10,000," he says to himself. "Salary alone
worth $9,000. Other $1,000 possible; let's check out his
debts." These are all now confirmed by TRW, and most
important, no new ones show up. "He's going to be
$13,000 in debt, if we give him the full loan. Shouldn't
be more than $11,200 . . . Let's see how he scored."

When he sees your total of 135, he nods. Gray area.
Very gray area.

"Any comment from the loan officer?" he wonders,
reaching for your application. There he reads about you
as a solid citizen, a person with business potential for
the bank.

"Possible," he mutters, "guy's a possible. Lot depends on his TRW." He starts flipping through the
sheets.

"Lots of folks giving him credit, been in the credit
market eleven years." He likes that, shows him you
have a history of being able to pay people back. "Mostly
everything is according to terms, couple sixty days late,
nothing to worry about."

Then he shifts to "Disputed Bills," a category that
matters to him. This is where you and Filene's are
trying to straighten out what really happened with that
sofa you returned.

On the bottom of your TRW report, the special
100-word message informs Jerry what is going on, what
Filene's claims, what you refute.

Such a report is not necessarily a black mark. Jerry knows that lots of people play games when it comes to disputed bills. They try to delay payments they know full well they legitimately owe or, maybe, through the sloppiness of their creditor, escape paying altogether.

But when Jerry looks at your TRW and sees two disputed bills on the whole thing, he shrugs. If he found a whole series of such disputes, he'd smell a dangerous pattern.

That kind of record is frequently connected with a whole series of closed accounts, which he checks next. On your record, he finds one oil credit card dropped after two years and nothing to indicate the reason was anything but lack of use. No fight with Mobil; you simply didn't use the card enough to make it worthwhile for them to carry you any longer.

What would alarm him is discovering a string of accounts, merchandise purchased, payments stretched out for six months or longer, payments finally made—under pressure, he knows—and then, account closed.

Jerry spends time with your TRW. He knows exactly how important it is. Now, he goes through your credit history again, this time trying to create a profile of you in his mind.

"Guy pays back according to terms, pretty much all along the way. Thirty days . . . thirty days . . . here's sixty days. When was that? Four years ago. How often? Twice, twice is all I see. No big deal . . . What's this one? Ninety days? Seven years ago, forget it. Look at all these thirty days . . . thirty days . . . steady as she goes, nice and regular. Seems like a good risk. Maybe, if Dave wants to stick his neck out, we can go over the limit a bit, lend them the full $10,000 . . . Whoops, what have we here?"

He has come to the great saga of you vs. Macy's. "One hundred and eighty days? Only three years ago. Got to be kidding. One hundred and eighty days, that's six months. Gotta know more about that one. Too big, too recent."

He calls Dave, your banker. You have already had

your chat with Dave, of course, fully briefed him on the whole Macy's charade. He is on your case and prepared to defend you, even to try and get you the full $10,000.

"Dave, we got two problems on this one," Jerry tells him. "I mean, I know you think highly of your customer . . ."

"Bad TRW?"

"Not so bad, except for one thing and it really troubles me," he replies. "Did you know that he went six months without paying Macy's?"

"That all you're worried about?"

"So far as the TRW is concerned."

"What else bothers you?" Dave asks. He might have to do some negotiating for you and wants to know what he's getting into. It's always possible that you were not completely honest with him, and even though he likes your business and wants you to be satisfied as a customer, he wants his own job protected much more. "You said there were two things bothering you, Jerry. What else?"

"Only other thing is the amount. Really, we should only be lending them $9,000. According to the guidelines."

"If that's it, then we have no problems," Dave says. "He explained that entire Macy's business to me. It was the standard screw-up, where he had moved, paid off everything, or so they thought, didn't get any further bills because Macy's kept sending them to the old address. Old story, my people only find out about the snafu when they go into the store about five months later, try to buy something, charge it, and practically find themselves under arrest. The whole thing was cleared up, and paid off quickly; once everything was straightened out. Showed me all the bills, checks, letter from their lawyer, everything."

"I don't find a memo on that here, Dave, in the folder."

"I'll get a letter from him right away."

"Better have it in the files," Jerry says. And adds absently: "That guy ought to ask Macy's to make a correction. Bad thing to be sitting in this TRW."

"Now, on the amount, I'll give you a memo on that

too. Those people are good for it. If we lend them $10,000, they'll pay it back just as surely as they'll pay back $9,000."

"Give me the memo, you got the loan," Jerry replies, happy to accommodate, so long as it's Dave's neck that's sticking out and not his own.

In fact, it's a small risk for Dave. He does have a relationship with you; he does expect more business from you; he does have reasonably solid credit information on you.

If Jerry had come up with more debt or more black marks, Dave might have dropped to the fallback position of $9,000, which you both had agreed to.

Or again, when tight money means tight loan policies, he might have had to tell you: "We can only lend you $9,000. Not so much a reflection on you as it is the economic climate . . ."

A perfectly legitimate qualification, but if you have doubts when you are told that, you can always go across the street and have a chat with a banker some friend of yours uses. Make an appointment with that man and see what he has to say about the "economic climate." If he confirms what Dave told you, take your $9,000 and redo your kitchen with only one coat of paint, instead of two.

If necessary, borrow a bank officer

It should be quite clear by now what most likely would have happened if you had not developed some sort of personal relationship with your banker and then, through that, been able to make him your informed advocate. Chances are you would have been turned down by Jerry: "Insufficient income" and "Delinquent credit obligations" he would have stamped, and they are perfectly good reasons for a rejection. Most important, he never would have taken the time to call Dave, your banker.

I had an experience recently that will be useful to you, just in case you find you need a loan, but you have not been able to develop any kind of personal contact yet with anyone in your bank.

You still need not go in cold and hope the computer will smile on you. You can borrow someone else's personal banking relationship.

Earlier this year, around the first of April, I got a call from a friend who wanted to help his friend. The man in need was a writer, working in films. The previous year, he had earned more than he ever had before, and like most people in that situation, he had not figured out more or less what his taxes would be on those earnings, so he had not put anything aside. Now his accountant had told him he had to pay the IRS nearly $25,000.

The fellow owned nothing. He rented his house in Brentwood, California. He leased both family cars. He was a self-employed freelance writer, which, as we know, is a terrible risk category for any bank. Yet he knew he would have to turn to a bank to save him from what he envisioned would be years on the chain gang.

At my friend's request, I called the fellow, Tom, and none too soon. That afternoon, he was about to go to his bank, and since he didn't know anyone in the place, his plan was to walk up to the desk farthest from the front door, which he assumed was the branch manager's desk, and ask the stranger for $25,000.

The branch manager, I told him, would resent his unannounced appearance, resent it very much. Probably enough to see to it that the loan was killed.

"But I don't know a soul in the bank," he said, nervously. "I've only been banking there a couple of years. What should I do, walk up to the guard and ask him who's giving out $25,000 loans today?"

I told him to keep away from the guard and asked him several questions. What did he have for collateral? What could he show the bank that would give them some reason to believe he could pay them back?

He had a "deal memo" and a letter from MGM

stating that he was to write a new film for them and that they would pay him $100,000 for doing so over the next year.

"Could you have whoever you're dealing with at MGM call the bank MGM uses?" I asked him. "One call like that, and you'd have the check in hours."

"I don't really have that kind of relationship with them," he replied. "My first film for them. I wouldn't feel right about that."

"Okay, what about your agent?"

"My agent? Lend me $25,000? That's really funny."

"No, no, not that he lends it to you, but he gets his bank to lend it to you."

"His bank? What's he got to do? Cosign the thing?"

"No, simpler than that. It won't cost him anything; he'll look good to his bank and do a great favor for his client," I told him. "One question: Is he a fairly substantial person, reputable, been an agent for a while?"

"Yeah, very solid. Has a number of big writers, also actors, directors. I'm the least successful client he has."

"All he has to do is take you into his bank and introduce you to the bank officer he does business with. And unlike yourself, you can be sure he does have someone. He explains the problem to that officer, tells him how solid you are, how you've got this $100,000 deal in hand, and all kinds of other, even bigger deals in the works, and I'm quite sure you'll get that loan."

"Sounds like magic."

"Not really. That banker doesn't look at your agent as just another account. That agent is a business. A business with growth potential. And that agent can bring that banker lots of new business, lots of clients who make very big bucks," I said. "Try it. It's a lot better than walking up to the bank guard."

Tom called his agent, who, as I expected, was delighted to do his client such a favor, especially at no cost or risk to himself. They went into his bank, spread it all out before his bank officer, and the next day, the bank officer had a check for Tom for $24,000, having explained to him that $25,000 was the limit of the authority she

had to lend on her own, and slightly under in this case
was slightly wiser.

So if you find yourself in a similar situation, borrow
somebody else's bank connection.

What to do, if the application is turned down

Let's look on the dark side of life.

Suppose, after all your efforts and nice talk with your
banker, your loan application was still turned down.

Do not curse and sigh and throw up your hands in
defeat. Do not, above all, decide that you have a flawed
character. Do not take the bank's decision in any way
personally. Their decision has absolutely nothing to do
with you as a human being, only with your numbers
and your credit history. You could be the warmest,
brightest, best-looking, most wonderful person in the
Western world and still be turned down for "Insufficient
income" and "Delinquent credit obligations."

Do not take the loan rejection, either, as if it were
some kind of final judgment, either on your value as a
member of the community, or your value as a credit
risk. You still have a number of possible moves.

First, of course, you have to pin your banker down
on the reason. Maybe you have no black marks on your
credit report, but you were simply asking for more
money than the 20 percent–25 percent ratios permit.
While this is the kind of thing you and your banker
should have caught beforehand, it could slip by.

In that situation, file a new application for less money.
The first rejection won't affect your new application and
its review, especially since this time, your banker will
be part of the plan.

If you try this, however, be sure your banker wants
to help. If you sense, instead, that he really doesn't
care, don't push it. You simply are not going to get your
money from that bank.

Go to a new bank. Use the technique and style we

discussed in Chapter 4. Get the name of an officer in that bank you can talk with and explain to him exactly what happened in your old bank. Tell him you wanted $10,000, but that was more than your numbers supported, which you didn't know when you applied. Explain further that you could live with $7,000, but make clear to him that you are getting absolutely no help from your previous banker on any of this. You will then represent two things to the new loan officer. First, you will seem like a good loan prospect for $7,000, and he always wants to make sound $7,000 loans. Second, he might be able to get you to shift all of your banking to his place.

If your loan was rejected for credit reasons, and you get your banker to tell you so, then follow up as we saw in Chapter 7. Get the name of the credit company, or companies, get on the phone, write letters, and get that credit report or reports. If you find mistakes, pursue them with the credit companies and the creditors, no matter how tedious it might be. You will not be able to get any loans, until you correct that report.

If in fact your credit report is dreadful, chock full of delinquent payments and disputed bills and closed accounts, then the sad truth is that no bank is going to lend you money. Not now. However, it is not the end of the world. I had a number of people looking for loans, who had just that problem, and the solution comes only with time.

Perhaps the most extreme case was a fellow who walked in one day and wanted a $5,000 loan. He filled out the application, omitting a few items, as I discovered the following day.

Credit in White Plains called. "John, where in hell did you find this guy?"

"Walk-in," I replied. "Never seen him before. Came in yesterday to open an account."

"I've never seen a TRW like this."

"Tell me about it," I said, genuinely surprised. The man had appeared to be perfectly respectable, well spoken, pleasant, all of which I knew could be deceptive, but still, the worst TRW ever?

"I don't think he ever paid anyone in less than a hundred and eighty days," the supervisor said. "He's got four creditors he made settlements with and apparently is still paying off; another two got judgments against him in court."

"Good lord."

"I mean that guy has a helluva lot of nerve walking through the front door, never mind asking you for five grand."

There was no answer at the number the man had put on the application, and I wondered if perhaps he was a disturbed person, if he would even bother to call me and inquire about the loan.

But that afternoon, he came in, looking fine, as pleasant as ever and sat down at my desk.

"I'm afraid I haven't got good news for you, Mr. Stevenson. Your loan application was rejected."

"May I ask why?"

"Your credit report, Mr. Stevenson. Frankly, it was terrible."

He nodded and rose to leave.

"Wait a minute, Mr. Stevenson; I wonder if I could talk to you about this."

He sat down again.

"There was an awful lot you didn't tell me or put on the application, Mr. Stevenson, and I must say I was somewhat surprised. I mean, you seem like an honest man."

"I am, Mr. Cook."

"Well, then, could you tell me, what's going on? I mean, surely you knew you didn't stand a chance of getting a loan with a credit report like that."

"I guess so."

"Mr. Stevenson, let me ask you something. And you're under no obligation to answer me. But I'm curious. On a kind of man-to-man basis, off the record, what happened? How did you get such a bad credit record?"

He paused. "I don't mind telling you, Mr. Cook, not for sympathy, but maybe you can tell me what I can do so I'm not such a pariah around banks."

He had quite a story. About four years ago, his son fell deathly ill. The kid was ten years old, struck with a rare blood disease, and at first given no chance to live.

Mr. Stevenson, obviously, was not a man to be easily turned aside. He searched around and found other doctors, who didn't offer great hope but thought there was some chance. They began treatment.

"For two years, all I did was pay doctors, Mr. Cook, no one else. I didn't have insurance to cover what they were doing, but I knew I had to find the money. I had my own business; I sold it. I had my own house; I sold it.

"I paid the doctors, and they kept my boy alive, and he's still alive, and we all think he's going to be alive for a long time.

"All during those years, my creditors kept calling. I never hid from anyone. I just didn't have any money for them, and I told them all why. Didn't matter to them, none of them. Didn't matter to me either. I mean, compared with my son's life, what did I care about my credit rating?

"The truth of the matter is I'd like to be able to start over. As you might realize, Mr. Cook, it's not easy getting along in our society if you have no credit. I'm sorry if I gave you any trouble, but I thought it was time for me to test the waters again, as I do from time to time. Obviously, they're not right for me, yet."

I believed the man. I've heard other stories like his. Sadly, there is no way the computers in any credit agency can make humane distinctions. And, I'm afraid there wasn't a great deal of comforting advice I could give him. The credit system is very rigid.

It would be three or four years before he would see any credit. Meantime, he did have a fairly good salaried job; he could support his family and their now more or less normal living expenses. He had to be absolutely certain to pay everything on time and grab the first piece of credit he could find.

Probably, that would be for a car, I told him. The easiest credit in the world comes from car dealers. They care much more about selling you their car than they do about your credit history. If you have a job, can make the down payment, are earning enough to pay monthly, and haven't gone into bankruptcy (which he had not), they'll take a chance on you. People meet their car payments, dealers know, because most people cannot survive without their cars.

So I pointed him toward a new car, told him to pay the thing off before it's due, and he'd be on his way back to respectability, so far as the credit world was concerned.

The other way around credit trouble is to use someone else's leverage with a bank. I recall one case in which a man was forced into bankruptcy, and so he acquired the worst of all credit marks.

The bankruptcy might have wiped him out financially, but it did not affect his skills in sales and marketing. Soon, he got himself a good new job, and soon after that, his boss, the owner of the company, came into the bank and made a special plea. "Do me a favor," he asked us. "He wants $10,000 of overdraft checking. He can't get it because of the trouble he had, but he's good for it today. It would mean a great deal to me if I could help him out here. This man is extremely valuable to me. My business is prospering as never before, since he joined us. Keep up like this, I'm going to make him a partner . . . I've been a good customer with you people for many years. Do me a favor . . ."

The fellow's personal and corporate business was too valuable to jeopardize. We extended the overdraft credit and kept a careful watch on it.

Checklist:

Plugging your banker into the loan process

1. Get and study your own credit report.
2. Review your application and chances for the loan with your bank officer, filling him in with good news and bad. Push him gently toward some favorable comments on his Application Transmittal form.
3. Arm him with information and give him a negotiating position to use on your behalf if he anticipates trouble.
4. If you don't get the loan, be certain to press for the real reason, especially if it's related to your credit report.
5. Get that report if you haven't already. If there are errors, get them cleared up and go back to your bank officer to review everything.
6. Reapply for the loan if he seems willing to back you. Otherwise, go to another bank . . . or forget it for now.

Chapter 10

Twelve varieties
of loans

What we've been considering in the previous two chapters is the most common kind of personal loan, a regular installment loan. Bankers like these because they are fairly uncomplicated, and they police themselves. You pay each month, and if you don't, a computer sends you a notice. Your banker doesn't have to bother calling you, doesn't have to keep track of the loan at all, while the bank receives its money in a regular, steady flow.

But you should know that there are other kinds of loans available to you, and some of them might be much more suitable than the installment plan, even if your banker is not quick to suggest them.

Demand loan

In theory, this is a loan on which the bank can "demand" payment at any time. In practice, that "demand" is rarely made. You and your banker agree on a time when you'll pay them back the principal of the loan, and that's what you strive to do. If you need an extension, you and your banker have another conversation.

Often there's nothing more than a memo from your banker in the file on this, no loan application, credit check, scoring or any of that stuff.

Obviously, your banker will make this kind of loan only to good customers he has known for some time, people he is confident are good for the risk.

If you're important and/or rich enough, he'll give you this loan without any collateral. Otherwise, he'll ask you to secure the loan by letting the bank hold on to a sufficient amount of your stocks and bonds until the loan is paid back.

That amount varies, according to government regulations.

I liked these loans because they were so flexible. They allowed me a chance to figure out the best plan for a customer's particular circumstances and to shape the loan around them.

Usually, these were people who had money coming to them in six months, a year, but needed help now. They might show me a will that was going to pay them a bundle next year, or contracts on jobs they had completed, where the last payment was not to be made for ten months.

Most often, I'd try to structure these demand loans so we'd get a certain amount paid to us during the course of the whole loan, though nothing like installment payments. If it were for $20,000, say, I'd ask the customer to pay us $2,000 in six months' time, another $2,000 six months later, another $2,000 six months after that. And, set up interest payments on a quarterly basis.

That way, if anything went wrong, we had at least brought the principal down to $14,000, from the original $20,000.

If their collateral was stocks and bonds, they had to

maintain their credit margin. If its value fell on the market, they'd have to give us more collateral, or pay down more on the loan in order to maintain their margin of, say, 70 percent.

Keeping the margin steady is one of the bothers with such a "stock and bond loan," as these are sometimes called. It was my job, as the bank officer who made them, to phone my customers for additional collateral when their stocks dropped. In 1974, when the market sank so badly, I was making calls every day to many of the same people.

The bank, remember, wants to collect its money from you. It does not want to have to "sell you out," get rid of the stocks and bonds in order to cover its loan. Chances are, if the bank has to do that, it won't collect its full amount, and it surely will rupture its relationship with you. Such an act also conjures images all bankers abhor, of the dreadful, wizened banker of the depression foreclosing on the destitute widow.

One problem some people have with demand loans is that the interest on them is often tied to the prime rate, and floats with it. If you get the loan at, say, prime-plus-two, that might start out being a total of 18 percent, which is high enough, to be sure. If the prime floats upward, so will your interest payments, always remaining at prime-plus-two.

Time note

This is basically the same as a demand loan, but it carries a firmer due date. You know you'll be getting a $20,000 bonus on December 20? Fine, let's make this due on December 27.

If there is some mixup, and the money is not paid to you on December 20, you tell your banker and he rolls the loan over with a new date. But those dates are meant to be firm. The payment, in other words, is not dependent on some "demand" on the part of the bank.

Evergreen loan

These are very special beauties in which your loan, it is understood, if never stated, will be rolled over and rolled over and rolled over, until you feel like paying it, or the bank finds itself in some kind of extremely tight position and is forced to call it in.

The name is appropriate, suggesting a perennial. Within the bank, it will be carried as a time note because regulations do not allow banks to make eternal loans. But with a wink and a handshake on this one, everyone knows just what will happen in ten months, when it supposedly comes due. You keep paying interest, and finally, when it suits your purposes, you pay it off.

At the moment, it's my impression that these lovely Evergreens are a thing of the past. Money is too expensive to allow them to flourish. But when times improve, banks will be accommodating their very best customers with such loans.

Small Business loan

This is a hybrid. The loan is not made to your business, or corporation; it is made to you, the small businessperson, and the "purpose of the loan" is your business. So you have to guarantee the loan, and show the credit to merit it, just as you would with any standard personal loan.

Because this is a special kind of loan, mixing business and personal elements, the way you deal with your banker and how you present your business to him are also special, and in the next chapter we'll consider it all.

Auto loan

This is the most common retail consumer installment loan and the easiest to get, because with this loan, the bank becomes co-owner of the car with you. Again, the last thing in the world a bank wants is to go into the used car business. But, it does know that the car is worth something, if worse comes to worst, so it does have some collateral.

So, even if you don't merit the amount you want, according to the regular scoring standards, and you don't show quite enough income according to 20 percent and 25 percent formulas, banks are very flexible with car loans.

With nearly all banks today, the processing of applications on car loans is completely automatic, but when it reaches Jerry, the credit reviewer, he has, as noted, much more margin for judgment than he does on other consumer loans. There could be black marks on your TRW credit report that would otherwise bother Jerry, but for this car loan, he shrugs.

A car dealer, as I noted earlier, will be even more lenient in his credit demands, but he'll probably charge you more interest.

A car loan is one loan where it makes sense to shop around. Because they are issued so mechanically, it doesn't matter whether you have a good relationship or none with a bank. And banks certainly use these loans to attract new business, with the result that you might find yourself saving $100 or more by dealing with a hungry bank.

Swing loan

This is a short-term loan that's used to "swing" you through a specific period and a special situation, most commonly between the selling and buying of homes.

You're moving to Denver. You've sold your house in Dallas, but the closing date isn't until March 10. Up in Denver, however, you're closing on a new house February 1.

For the down payment, you need the money from the sale in Dallas to pay for Denver. Usually, all your bank requires is to see the two contracts, and they'll lend you what you need, confident they will be repaid as soon as the paper work in Dallas is completed.

Mortgages

Though most people think of mortgages as something else, they are in fact loans made against your house. After doing its credit check on you, and perhaps appraising the house, the bank decides to lend you a substantial amount of money, for a long period of time, and covers its risk in part by owning the house with you.

Traditionally, this area of the banking business has belonged to savings institutions, with commercial banks making mortgages only as a very special convenience to their very special customers. Today, with so many savings institutions in such trouble, an increasing number of commercial banks are nervously picking up mortgage business.

If you want a mortgage, and your commercial bank doesn't make them, talk to your banker anyway about a bank that does. He can be extremely helpful in recommending you to another bank, and for this kind of unique loan, he shouldn't be afraid that he'll be losing your other business. Quite the contrary.

Not only will his recommendation allow you to establish the desired businesslike relationship with the new banker, but your commercial banker's comments on you as a customer will carry considerable weight with the new savings fellow.

Bankers trust each other for this kind of recommendation. In fact, the degree of trust even surprised me recently, when I made just such a call to a savings bank for one of my customers. There was no question in my mind this man should be given the mortgage he was after, and I told the other bank officer all about him in glowing terms. The fellow thanked me, and when I offered to put my comments in a letter to him, he said that wouldn't be necessary. My comments confirmed their own impression of the applicant, and they were now going to issue the mortgage. Our phone conversation of a bit more than five minutes locked up $75,000 for my customer. Simple as that.

Because mortgages involve such large sums for such long periods of time, typically fifteen to thirty years, getting the best possible deal can save you hundreds, maybe thousands of dollars. So shop around, and don't be afraid to negotiate. A bank's interest rates on a mortgage are not cast in stone.

These days it is common for banks to tack "points" onto a mortgage. A "point" is one percent of the amount you're borrowing. If you're asking for a mortgage of $50,000, a "point" will be $500. Try to negotiate those out of your deal. They are usually easier to undo than the interest rate itself.

Also try to negotiate a mortgage without a prepayment penalty, or, a minimal one. With interest bouncing around these days, you want to be able to make an adjustment without paying dearly for it.

Assume you get the $50,000 mortgage and you can't do any better than, say, a 16 percent rate. In twenty months, thanks to miracles, you see interest rates dropping to 12 percent. That's when you want to go in and have another chat with your mortgage banker. Don't expect him to call you because he's perfectly happy having you pay 4 percent more than the existing market.

Before seeing him, call or visit a few of the banks advertising the 12 percent rate and satisfy yourself that you could, if you wanted, take out a new mortgage from one of them at the new, lower rate.

With that information in hand, visit your mortgage

banker, and tell him you'd like to pay up your original mortgage and take out a whole new mortgage with him, but at the new rate. Since he's a businessman, he should realize that if he doesn't give you what you want, you'll go to one of his competitors.

This is where the prepayment penalty comes in. It is intended first, to cover the bank's expenses in writing up and processing your mortgage. The penalties, however, add up to much more than the few hundred dollars it might cost in somebody's time and whatever is involved in opening up a new mortgage file.

The excess goes to the bank as a form of compensation. When they gave you the mortgage, they expected to realize a certain return over a period of years. These days that might be 15 percent for fifteen years. If you pay it off after a year, they want some compensation, and that's the prepayment penalty.

Some states now prohibit them on mortgages, others limit the amounts banks may charge you to something between three and six months in interest. Normally, these penalties are only applied if you prepay in the first year of the mortgage. So, it's best to wait out that time, then renegotiate.

In practice, what you are doing is taking money from the new mortgage, and this time, instead of giving it to the seller of the house as you did the first time around, you give it to the bank that made your original mortgage.

On your $50,000 mortgage, in twenty months you will have paid off very little of the principal of the loan. Let's say you still owe $49,500 on it. That's the amount you take on your new mortgage, and that's what you hand over to your old bank. Obviously, if you renegotiate with the same bank for a new, lower mortgage rate, no money or checks change hands. It's all paper work and bookkeeping.

Knowing that you are not locked into a high interest rate should relieve some of your interest anxiety. Everyone has it, and people are always trying to outguess the interest market in deciding when they'll buy a house.

Of course, the amount of interest you pay greatly affects the amount of your monthly mortgage payment. And you might find yourself unable to buy at a given time because interest rates have pushed those payments up beyond your ability to pay.

However, if you can make the payments, you should not decide to wait on buying a house simply because rates are high. I think that's crazy, and I have always told my customers that if they need a house, and they've found one they really like, and they can get a fair price on it, which they can afford, they should buy it. If they wait for interest rates to drop, inevitably they'll lose the house, and/or they'll be faced with yet higher, not lower interest rates. Buy the house. Then, if the rates really drop, get a new mortgage.

Second mortgage

Your first mortgage was $50,000, and that plus $20,000 you put down in cash bought you the house you wanted for $70,000.

That was ten years ago, and since then, doing nothing to your house but keeping it upright, painting a bit here and there, and living in it happily, you've seen its value go up and up and up. You now have a house that real estate brokers tell you confidently they could sell for $125,000.

That news makes you feel good, but it doesn't help much when you decide you don't want to sell your house, all you'd like to do is add on a room.

Unfortunately, the same inflation that has helped to push up the value of your place also has forced the cost of that new room up to $15,000. "One room," you mutter, "for $15,000. Practically my entire down payment on the entire house."

A second mortgage is one way you can pay for your expansion. With it, the bank will appraise the present value of your home, deduct the amount you still owe on your first mortgage, and lend you money on a portion of what's left.

In your case, if the value has truly risen to $125,000, which means the bank's appraisal agrees with that of your neighborhood real estate agent, the bank will subtract the amount you still owe on your $50,000 mortgage from the new value of the house. Let's say you still owe $40,000. According to the bank, then, your equity in the house is $85,000 (the $40,000 you still owe on your mortgage subtracted from the house's new value of $125,000). That's what you could walk away with, if you sold it today.

The bank will make its loan against the $85,000. Usually $15,000 is tops for a second mortgage. The loan will be for a long stretch, five to ten years, so the monthly payments would be low, considerably more manageable than if you had borrowed your $15,000 on a regular consumer installment loan.

Commercial banks almost never make second mortgages, but savings institutions and finance companies do. Once again, you've got to shop around.

Though second mortgages are typically used for home improvements, they don't have to be. In recent years, for example, I have seen a number of people secure second mortgages on their homes to help finance their children's college educations.

Refinancing your mortgage

You might find yourself in a situation where the value of your home goes up and up, you don't want to sell the house, yet you need capital. I'm not talking about money to visit China, or to buy a second car, or any of the things you would normally cover with savings or a consumer loan.

Perhaps you have an opportunity to buy into a business, or start your own business. Perhaps, and this is trickier, you have a good financial adviser and he or she works out a sophisticated long-range plan that will let you retire and have $50,000 a year rolling in, if you can make some substantial investments this year.

The capital you are looking for is sitting in the increased value of your home. Let's say that amounts to $75,000. You can go to the bank that gave you your mortgage seven years ago at 9 percent and tell them you'd like to refinance. They'll be interested because refinancing means a new mortgage at the current rates, say, 16 percent.

They'll base this new mortgage on the new, increased value of your house. It's now worth $150,000, up from $75,000, when you bought it? Fine, they'll figure a new mortgage based on that $150,000. If they are requiring 20 percent down payments on their mortgages, that means $30,000. If you were coming in to actually buy the house, you'd have to produce $30,000 cash, and they'd lend you $120,000 as the mortgage.

In this case, you would have up to $120,000 you could borrow, using your house as collateral. Your interest rates would leap. If you were paying 9 percent and the going rate is 16 percent, your bank will be so happy to wipe that 9 percent loser from its books, you can probably negotiate something closer to 14 percent with them. Your monthly payments will increase accordingly.

You'd suddenly have $120,000 to invest, or do with as you wanted. But you'd also have those enormously higher carrying charges. So, you have to be extremely careful, if you consider refinancing, and be sure that you aren't leading yourself into a situation you can't afford. If you cannot sustain all those additional new costs, you're going to lose your house.

I recall being laughed at about five years ago at a Los Angeles party. Everyone there was refinancing their homes. Inflation and an exploding real estate market had suddenly made their $50,000 homes worth $200,000, $300,000. Why, they'd be fools not to grab that found money while they could, they told me. It's all funny money, I warned them, funny money going up and hilarious money when it comes down. I wouldn't lend you a penny against your houses. That's phony equity you're looking at.

They called me a stuffy New York banker and worse, and they refinanced. Several of those people have since been forced to sell their homes, even default on the inflated mortgages. They took their "found money," made bad investments with it, and instead of having income from those investments to cover their heavy new mortgage costs, they collapsed.

So refinancing is something to consider, but only with the advice of your accountant, possibly your lawyer, your financial adviser, as well as your banker.

If it does make sense for you, I should warn you that you cannot always find banks willing to do it. If there is not a great deal of money around, your bank's policy might be to make mortgage loans only to people who want to buy homes, not to people like you who are trying to create capital.

Condominium and cooperative loans

Among the differences between condos and coops are the ways banks look at them when it comes to mortgages.

With a condominium, you buy the unit itself, much as you would be buying an individual house.

With a cooperative, however, you are not buying the unit, you are buying shares in a corporation that owns your unit and all the others in that building.

A bank will lend you money in a mortgage to buy your condo, and the terms will be quite like the mortgage they would give you if you were buying a house.

But with a coop, a bank will not give you a mortgage, because technically speaking, you are not buying a piece of real estate that you can then use as collateral on their loan. If you cannot make the payments, all they can do is sue you, and/or take possession of the shares in the coop you own. Then they have to abide by the many rules of your coop. They have to pay your monthly maintenance fees while they're trying to sell your coop in order to get the money back you still owe them. And when they find a buyer, that buyer has to meet all the standards set by the cooperative.

If you cannot make payments on your condo, they can repossess it and sell it, just as they would do with a house.

Coops, then, are somewhere in limbo, and banks have concocted limbo loans. Basically, this is a personal loan, but for a large amount and for a long period of time. It will be slightly more expensive than a mortgage, but less expensive than a regular personal loan. It will be for somewhat less time than a mortgage, but much longer than a regular personal loan.

Passbook loans

If you have a passbook savings account, you can make a loan against a portion of your savings, and the interest you'll be charged will be quite low—about four to five percentage points above what your savings account is earning if you have it in a savings institution. Commercial banks used to charge about six percentage points above the interest they were paying to savings accounts. But in today's market, their interest rates on these loans are almost as high as those on their other, consumer loans.

Most of the time, however, you're better off simply taking the money out of your savings account. Assuming that you have a good reason for the money, use your savings and avoid paying all the interest you'd have to pay the bank on a loan for the same amount. If you do that, be certain that you have some kind of forced savings plan, so that you'll replenish your savings, and not leave yourself without a rock.

I've known people who didn't trust themselves to put the money back in their savings accounts. They would have no trouble paying off a regular installment loan on schedule, they assured me. But, for whatever reason, they were hopeless when it came to savings. It was an absolute miracle that they had managed to put away what they had. Or, maybe not such a miracle: Maybe everything in their savings account came from a single bequest, a single gift from someone who died.

With those people, I told them to take the passbook loan. They were punishing themselves with those interest costs, but on the other hand, they would sleep at night.

Checklist:

Twelve Varieties of loans

1. Demand loan
2. Time note
3. Evergreen loan
4. Small business loan
5. Car loan
6. Swing loan
7. Mortgage
8. Second mortgage
9. Refinancing your mortgage
10. Condominium and cooperative loans
11. Passbook loans

Chapter 11

Advice for
the small
businessperson

I used to enjoy making loans to small businessmen and businesswomen. Unlike so much of banking, there was nothing mechanical about these loans. Each one required a great deal of involvement on my part and personal judgment, and when they worked, there was a real measure of personal satisfaction as well. Often, one of these loans could make a great difference in a company's success.

These are not simply corporate loans cut down. They are not loans to corporations or businesses at all. They are loans to individuals, who have to guarantee them, and who are going to put the money into their businesses. So it meant I had to understand enough about the business to pass some judgment on its chances, and I had to know enough about the individual to pass further judgment.

Make a loan to IBM; you are not making it to the officers or the shareholders, but to an entity. It's big bucks, but a fairly mechanical analysis is all you need.

You've got a hardware store, or a small factory that manufactures metal coasters, some kind of business where the volume of sales is less than $1 million? You're much tougher, when it comes to a loan decision. Also, much more interesting.

First, get organized

That might seem obvious, advising you to be organized, but so many small businesses are fairly improvised operations. One man or woman has some general goals, an idea of what he's making or selling, what his market is, how he'd like to do better, and then it's day by day, making decisions as he goes along, cutting corners, making compromises, somehow getting from point A to point B, and earning a living.

But that style of juggling will not impress your banker. He wants to see you in control. He wants to have confidence in you, and only you can instill it. What I advised earlier about being businesslike when it comes to your personal banking applies ever more here.

I had small businesspeople plop down at my desk and say: "I think I'm going to need $35,000 in about two weeks." They had no clear figures to support that amount. Often, they were heading for a rough stretch, but they simply had not anticipated the problems, which a bit of discussion revealed were chronic problems for their business.

These folks made me uneasy. If I knew them well, I'd send them off to think through their needs and pull together the information I required for a decision. Otherwise, I sent them off with little hope that they'd get their money from us.

Deep in his mind, your bankruptcy

When you approach your banker, never forget that, in fact, small businesses are terrible risks. What is deepest in your banker's mind is that he's going to make a loan, for which he'll undoubtedly have to put himself on the line, and then you'll go bankrupt. You have to remove his fears, and there are several ways you can do it.

The first is to be impressively organized. Be sure of what you want, why, and when you'll be able to pay it back.

Continually throughout this loan process, your banker is measuring you. Remember, he is making the loan to you, not your company. He'll ask you all kinds of questions about your business, and he'll examine all your books. But more important than the business itself is the way you explain it to him. Do you make sense? Can you explain the numbers of your business to him so that he feels you really know what you're talking about?

He'll know enough about your business to assess it, even if he won't know enough to run the business himself. If he decides, for example, that you are paying far too much for those commissioned sales reps, way higher than the industry average, he will worry about where you're going to get the capital to pay him back. Or, eventually, if you can stay in business at all.

But all his business judgments are filtered through his personal screen.

This can be played out in subtle ways. Whenever I reviewed projections with a small businessperson, I could see that they were always optimistic projections. But that's okay. How could anyone ever start a small business, unless he was an optimist?

Assuming that the projected numbers were not completely ridiculous, what I always wanted to see was some realization that maybe everything would not go as planned. Maybe there would be troubles. Maybe, in fact, the business wouldn't work. Obviously, I didn't expect anyone to come to me and say: "Well, I'll probably be bankrupt in six months, but meanwhile, could you help me out with $50,000?" But some honest awareness that life was tough and risk was always with us was meaningful to me.

Was my customer capable of being honest with himself, of being dispassionate about his business chances? Sometimes not. Sometimes, all they saw were blue skies, and those people had a very tough time getting a loan out of me.

Keeping in touch

The better I knew my small business customers, the better their chances for loans. This was no place for strangers. I wanted to hear from these people regularly. I wanted to know how business was going, even when they didn't owe us anything. I wanted to lunch with them a couple of times a year, so we could have a chance to talk for a couple of hours in a fairly relaxed way.

If they did owe us money, communication was even more important. The computer would tell me that Mr. Miamo was making his payments on time. What I wanted to hear from him was how tough it was for him to be making those payments.

Most of all, I wanted to be ahead of trouble. I said earlier that a banker's greatest fear with a small business loan is that the company will go bust. But that doesn't happen overnight. There are warning signals and patterns. In fact, I never had a bankruptcy occur on any of my small business loans. But I always harbored the fear, and I always figured that as long as I could be talking with the hustling man or woman I had lent the money to, I could know if real trouble was developing.

There were times when the news was not so bright, and I was able to help out. I could dispassionately analyze some of the problems, often cash flow problems, or undercapitalization so common to small businesses. Sometimes we had to stretch out the loan. Sometimes I had to point out to the owner that he really needed a partner, someone who could invest capital in return for a share of the company. The bank, I had to remind him, was not a partner. We did not own or want a share of the business. We wanted our loan repaid, with interest.

Silence was frightening to me. It'll scare your banker too.

The five-part written proposal

When it comes time for a loan, your banker needs more than talk. He's going to have to convince his boss, perhaps the branch manager, to approve the loan, so you have to prepare him to argue your case. Give him all the material he needs in a written proposal, and it should be put together around five areas.

1. *Your banker needs a very clear description of your business.* It can be brief, but it must be detailed. What is your product? How do you make your profit? Why are you in that business?

One of the engaging things about small businessmen and businesswomen is that they're immersed in their work. They love and hate it; they live it day and night. But this same quality can hurt them, when it comes to a loan, because they assume that their banker knows and cares as much about their business as they do. Not so.

In this first part of your presentation, walk your banker through your operation. It'll not only clarify your work for him, but he might want his boss to read your proposal to familiarize him, before he makes his own pitch on your behalf. I found that useful, but only, of course, when the proposal was clear and complete.

2. *Next, give him a description of yourself in relation to the business.* What were you doing before this

business? What education do you have, what professional training and experience that makes you especially suitable for this particular work? How did you happen to get into this business?

Let me warn you that one of the things your banker will be wondering is whether or not you are suited for your business. In other words, is the real purpose of this loan to bail you out of a big mistake? Is this the wrong business for you?

3. *Then, provide a historical analysis of your business.* If it was already in existence and you took it over, when was that and what shape was the business in then? What has happened since? If you started the company, what were your business reasons for doing so? What was the market environment when you started out? What were your projections when you started, and how have they turned out?

How much of your own money have you invested in the business? This is extremely important to your banker. It not only indicates the kind of commitment you've made, but if your investment is substantial and meaningful in terms of your net worth, it is an assurance to your banker that you'll fight to be successful. If things go sour, you won't run away from trouble, or go bankrupt rather than struggle.

You want to present yourself as someone who knows what he's doing, but someone who's been lucky. Your projections and financial statements since you've been in business, or at least for the last three years, should help.

With a new business, you'll have a tougher time normally getting a loan. If you've been going for only a year and you need more capital, your banker is going to tell you you didn't get enough capital together before you opened shop. He might recommend that you find an investor now, or if you have stocks and bonds, that you consider selling them and investing the proceeds in your company. You might be able to get a personal loan from him, but if your income is coming from your company, as is likely, he'll ask you to secure the loan with personal assets of some sort.

4. *Credit references*. Give him your personal credit information and a financial statement of your own net worth.

Also provide him with the names of two or three of your suppliers. They are your best credit references, for they'll show him how solid you are and how you pay your bills. Assuming that you have reasonably good relationships with these suppliers, they will be only too happy to report good news about you. A loan to you and your business can only mean more business for them.

5. *Finally, the amount and specific purpose of the loan*. Exactly where will the money go? Plant expansion? New equipment? Additional employees? Spell it out, showing what your costs will be.

Though you have separate projections that you provide your banker, give him here an idea of what his loan can do for your business. If it is for plant expansion, talk briefly about the new capacity you'll have and how that will improve your total picture. What your banker wants to see is a good possibility that you'll grow. "They might be small now," I used to tell my boss, "but everything they show me indicates that they won't stay small. They'll grow, and our business with them should grow accordingly." It's the same as we saw with personal banking: One of the questions always running through the banker's mind is, what's the potential for growth here? Give him plenty of solid reason for hope.

If you don't get the loan, be certain to talk it over with your banker. Get the reason for the rejection, bearing in mind that there were several people reviewing your case. What troubled them?

In a critical way, these loans are different from the usual personal loan. They are more essential. So often I found that people rejected for personal loans simply made do. They waited, or they applied for a smaller amount and scaled down their plans.

But a small business loan had better be essential, or the banker will quickly decide that the small business-person doesn't know what he's doing. If there is a real need for capital, however, then rejection could badly jolt the company. You've got to go to another bank and try again, and you've got to do it armed with the reason for your rejection. The second time around, somehow you're going to have to anticipate the same worry on the part of your new banker.

If you do have to look elsewhere, tell the new banker that you're prepared to move all your banking business to him if he can get you the loan you're after now. You don't want to become a "bouncer," of course, but if you can't get the business support you need from your present bank, what good are they?

However, don't make the move until they come up with your loan. Bankers play games with small business-men, fishing games, and the bait, of course, is the promise of the desperately needed loan. Make them produce before you leap. As I noted earlier, the new banking legislation of October 1982 will permit savings banks to issue business loans for the first time. It will be a while before they are equipped and staffed for those loans, but when they are, go talk to them. Their money will be just as green as the stuff in a commercial bank, and since they'll be new to the field, they might be hungrier for your loan business.

Checklist:

Writing a proposal for a small business loan

1. Give your banker a clear, detailed description of your business. What it is you make or sell. How your business works and you make your profit.
2. Provide a description of yourself in relation to the business. What were you doing before this? What training, experience, education makes you especially suitable for this work?
3. A historical analysis of your business. Was it a going business, or did you start it? What was it like when you began? What projections did you have then? How have you actually done?
4. Credit references, personal and business.
5. The amount and specific purpose of the loan, and how it should improve your business.

Chapter 12

Who they
really are

Most people have a stereotype of bankers. Upper-class, button-down, WASP, haughty, arrogant, aloof, icy, very Ivy League, very conservative, with all the sensitivity and sense of humor of a freshly painted wall.

I must confess that there is a certain amount of accuracy in that widespread perception. It's a damning confession, certainly. But, any banker with half a brain knows that is how he or she is perceived by the public. That's why so many banks spend millions of dollars to convince you otherwise.

Just think of all the TV ads you're constantly seeing in which the banker looks like a wonderful, warm human being, absolutely killing himself to be nice. He's being nice to old folk who are confused, or to Chinese folk who don't speak much English, or to women in a hurry, or to railroad conductors who have to start work at six A.M., or to guys on the waterfront at the fish market who have to start at four A.M. Like some totally compassionate, all-understanding, all-helpful Supreme

Being, he's being nice to His whole flock—white folk, black folk, yellow folk, young and old, rich and poor, all creeds and religions... You can just hear the faintly martial-spiritual music in the background.

Then, you go into your own bank, and you find yourself kind of looking around, without even meaning to, searching for a face that resembles the glowing countenance of the banker on your TV set. But, surprise, surprise, you do not find him.

What is your banker really like? Well, as with most things in life where human beings are concerned, the truth is not black and white, it is gray.

WASP power

One of the truths of your cliché has to do with WASPs. It is fair to say that the greatest amount of power and control of banks in America today resides with WASPs.

It is also fair to say that the WASP sensibility, the WASP style and manner, the WASP approach to money, people, and life is the predominant influence on our major banks.

Not everyone who works in a bank today is or must be a white, Anglo-Saxon, Protestant male graduate of an Ivy League school. Once, the profession above the level of clerk was pretty much ascribed to people with those qualities.

Until recently, say twenty years ago, banks were nice places for rich boys to go after Yale or Princeton, especially if they weren't terribly bright, or ambitious. Sort of like entering yet another acceptable school or club. Most respectable, certainly, offering the veneer of a job in High Finance, and all the heady aura that that conveys, while at the same time not being too strenuous.

Further, it often meant going into the family business, a warm and happy tradition. It was not so long ago that wealthy families either owned great gobs of stock in a bank, or deposited such disproportionately substantial sums that they assumed proprietary interest in the whole bank. "Our bank... has been for generations...." When Tad finished Princeton, barely, Dad installed him behind a desk in Our Bank.

To be sure, this was not a desk out there on the floor, the kind of desk you see when you go to do your banking, the kind of desk I had. You never saw Tad, certainly never approached his desk nervously for your piddling loan. You approached me. Tad's desk was somewhere upstairs, or downtown, in the Trust Department where he only saw people like himself, and from the bank's point of view, hopefully saw them in such a way that they would also bring their WASP millions into the bank.

To a degree, that has not changed. The heirs to those invisible WASP fortunes—quiet, vast fortunes that reach back generations and centuries, which the public never hears about—those heirs, especially the underachievers, still are placed behind desks in Trust. You never see them, you never deal with them. For you and your car loan, there are more normal people, folks who might even be, like me, an Irish Catholic poor boy from Brooklyn, or these days—*mirabile dictu*—blacks, or women even.

In fairness, I should admit that there are some limits. The son of one man who owned a medium-sized New York bank used to come to work every morning, put his feet up on his desk, his very clean desk, and read the morning papers. Then he'd go out to lunch. After lunch, he'd come back and put his head down on his desk and take his nappy. Then he'd wake up and go home. That was it, a full day's work, day after day, another day, another dollar. Sadly, Daddy sold the bank to a larger bank, a grown-up mean bank, and soon they asked Daddy if he wouldn't mind finding another form of employment for Junior, or at least another place for him to nap. As I said, there are limits.

In fact, I had an experience that further verified the ways things are changing, and, one might even say, indicated a certain democratization in the world of banking.

I remember a fellow in the Trust Department, whom I'll call Parkinson Talbot. So far as the bank was concerned, Talby's best qualities were that he was worth about $10 million himself, and he had this terrific lockjaw, WASP accent. It is the perfect accent when dealing with rich old ladies around New York.

It is not, interestingly, a useful accent for someone in the Corporate Division, because it would be offensive to so many corporate types who represent lots of money and business for the bank, even though they have no WASPness in their blood, and speak like you or me.

Also, such an accent would be offensive to many people outside the East. Talby would not be very successful, for example, selling the bank's investment research to other banks in California, where bankers would shudder, thinking, "It's jerks like that we were fleeing from when we moved out here."

The senior officers who ran our bank, just as their shrewd counterparts in other good banks, would automatically recognize the pluses and minuses of Talby and keep him with his own kind. They would make such a decision and assignment, furthermore, without so much as a word being exchanged among them. Automatic as a computer.

The perfect accent for banking, by the way, is Walter Cronkite's, essentially transcendent, without a specific regional tone from any place, absolutely all-American. (Come to think of it, Cronkite, with that air of trust, honesty, dependability, fairness, and decency he projects, is in many ways a terrific model for bankers.)

As it was, despite my Brooklyn origins, I was presentable enough for the bank to actually let me meet rich folk customers, under the supervision, of course, of Lockjaw Talby.

One day, a Mrs. Winthrop came into the bank to have lunch with Talby and me and to review some of her investments.

Before going into the private dining room, we were

sitting in Talby's office, waltzing through a bit of the basic preliminary social chatter. The woman was most pleasant and, like so many from old rich families I met, in no way pretentious or intimidating. There was even a kind of extra warmth and gentleness in her, perhaps growing out of her deep security.

She told us about her drive in from Long Island and the traffic, and then she asked Talby where he lived. He replied, through his closed teeth, "Greenwich." Perfect answer.

Then she turned to me. "And tell me, John, where do you live?"

Well, the truth was Brooklyn. But, before I could say that terrible word, Talby interjected: "John lives in Long Island, Mrs. Winthrop." He smiled, now baring those clenched teeth, and quickly added: "Perhaps we should head down to lunch?"

She ignored him. "Oh, isn't that nice, John," she said, smiling warmly at me. "So do I. We live in Westbury. What part do you live in?"

It was clearly my question. Talby glanced sharply at me, and I got his message. "Bay Ridge," I replied, which was the truth, Bay Ridge being part of Brooklyn, even though it connoted a hamlet in the south of England.

"Bay Ridge?" she said. "Bay Ridge? Isn't that odd. I don't think I've ever heard of Bay Ridge, John. Where in Long Island is it? It sounds perfectly lovely."

"It's very close to the city, Mrs. Winthrop," I answered, again speaking only the truth, if dissembling in a way that somewhat betrayed my Jesuit education. To be sure, I didn't say just a bridge away, but then there was no need for that much candor.

Talby smiled, nodded at me with some admiration. I was happy to follow him and Mrs. Winthrop to lunch.

Talby had the accent, as we saw, and the $10 million. He really didn't need to work, but it would have been socially unacceptable for him to be unemployed. His job was hardly demanding, certainly no one expected great financial wisdom or expertise from him. He had barely managed to graduate from Brown, where Dad had gone, needless to say, and no one at the bank had any illusions about his potential.

All things considered, I felt there were not a lot of businesses that would have hired Talby. But, I figured, given the way of the WASPs, he had nothing to worry about.

I was wrong. One day, I heard that Talby had actually been fired.

I would never have thought that could ever happen, not to good old Lockjaw Talby with his perfect accent and his $10 million. And perhaps ten years earlier it would not have happened. But I realized, on hearing the news, that times had changed somewhat. In fact, Talby got another job at another bank. But I knew that our bank had become, first and foremost, a business, a serious business.

It's not enough to be a rich WASP, I thought, when I heard the news of Talby that afternoon. Not anymore.

The feel of solidity

If all that's so, you might ask, and things have really changed and it's not enough to be a WASP anymore, then how come everyone in the bank you use still *seems* to be a WASP? Even the "minority" women they've hired so recently? And why do banks *feel* so WASPy, like Westminster Abbey?

Good questions. Let me try to answer the last one first, about the feel of the place.

A lot of that is in the eye of the beholder. Banks do try to reflect the appearance of solidity and permanence of an enduring institution. The reason is obvious: to gain your trust.

There's an interesting historical motive here. One hundred to a hundred and fifty years ago, banks had a bad name. They were frequently storefront operations, unregulated, often set up by well-dressed con artists.

They won the trust of people, conned them into handing over their money for safekeeping, then folded their banks and fled in the night.

That is not such a hot image for a banker, a con artist who is here today and gone tomorrow with your money.

Toward the end of the nineteenth century, when banks were being regulated and coming under minimal controls of federal law, they became more permanent, more dependable, even more honest.

To signify their new character, they began to design their places of business, to symbolize their new upright character. They built large, solid, institutional structures, many even suggesting cathedrals. Trust in the Lord for your spiritual needs and your banker for your temporal needs, these mercantile cathedrals seemed to be saying.

That attempt at image lifting through edifice was aided by a coincidental movement in American architecture at the beginning of the twentieth century. The surge was to the grandiose. Quite naturally, banks got bigger and more imposing, humbling their customers more and more. I find it fascinating to drive through small towns all over America and see how often the biggest, maybe the only truly imposing structures in the town are the churches and the banks.

Only recently has the trend been stalled. Once again, reality prevails. Banks are no longer the domain of the few. They are serious businesses. As such, image or not, they have to face the cost per square foot of building these days, or the cost per square foot of renting in downtown these days, or the cost of heating or cooling those three-storied shrines.

So the cathedral effect is diminished in the smaller suburban branch bank, but still the tone is the same. Quiet, reserved, institutional. And, of course, in the spacious beauties of old, ever more so.

I think that most of us associate those subdued qualities with WASPdom. The WASPs, as your cliché has it, are supposed to be reserved, icy, button-downed. And that's the feel of your bank, which is one reason you think everyone in it is a WASP breathing out some

magic WASP carbon dioxide that affects your vision and
your mind when you enter the hushed shrine. You step
into your bank's arched nave, and suddenly, the whole
world is WASP.

Supply-side WASPness

There is another reason, another answer to your
question. Though it is true that one does not have to be
a WASP to work in and make substantial progress in a
bank today, it is also true that at the top, WASPs still
reign. And from the highest levels, their WASPness has
a way of seeping down and permeating everyone and
everything in the bank. Call it supply-side WASPness.

In fact, if you want to get ahead in a large bank, as I
did, you feel the pervasive pressure to mimic them.

That's why the assistant treasurer, a black woman,
somehow comes across to you, incredible as it seems,
projects to you across her desk, an aura of WASPness.
Consciously or unconsciously, she knows the way her
boss, a genuine WASP, walks, talks, dresses, acts. And
it's her boss who's going to have a lot to say about her
progress in the bank, about the raises she gets, the
promotions and bonuses she receives. She knows,
consciously or unconsciously, she had better please
him.

The game of Mimic the WASP—which incidently
goes on in countless businesses with a number of
variations, all of which add up to Mimic the Boss—the
game in the bank is played in countless ways. And, I
learned, it has to be played with care and skill.

Two rules of the game

1. You can't be too obvious about your mimicking;
and,

2. Acting like a WASP is not in itself enough to
assure progress.

When I first joined the bank, I told you, I was put through a training program that involved observing and working in several departments.

In the Securities Service Department, I sat at a desk next to a fellow who was a couple of years younger than I, but he didn't look like me or anyone else in the whole office. He looked older.

He wore a Brooks Brothers suit, a Brooks Brothers button-down white shirt, Brooks Brothers wing-tipped shoes. All the rest of us wore what I considered at the time more normal clothes. Colored shirts, fat ties, regular shoes from Tom McAn.

As you might have guessed, at that point in my life, I had not seen a lot of WASPs, never mind worked with them. But what confused me even more about this fellow was that his name was O'Brien.

Several months later, I was discussing my training program with a personnel officer. Mainly, he asked lots of questions about the various departments I had moved through. It was a way for him to evaluate the program as well as the people who worked in the different departments.

At one point, he asked me about Securities Service. I told him what I had been doing there, what I thought I learned, and then I remembered John O'Brien.

"Oh, by the way, I heard the other day that John O'Brien has left the bank. He was the person I was working with most there."

"Yes, O'Brien," he said, watching me. "What did you think of him?"

I shrugged. "I don't know. Perfectly nice to me. Helpful."

"Hmmm. Well, he didn't fit in."

"Yes," I replied, thinking I understood his remark. "He did seem different somehow from everyone else in the office there."

He smiled slightly. "We had some problems with O'Brien. Unfortunate. But he just didn't perform up to the job. Pity." He paused and looked over to the side and spoke, almost as if to himself. "You know, frankly, he tried to be like us, talk like us, everything, but he just didn't have it."

Being a pseudo-WASP just isn't enough.

As I was to discover, in fact they would prefer for you to be their best son, from the best school, best family, best Protestant church, that you dress right, talk right, be imbued by God with all the best stuff.

But if you are not, that's still okay, to certain limits. If you are not, but you can effect certain adaptations, and produce for them, do the job, they will reward you. In the name of propriety, they do want you to play the Mimic the WASP game in a certain way, which includes at the least dressing and acting in their conservative style.

If you do that, and in addition are willing to slave to get degrees at night, go to business school as I did for seven years of nights, they will reward you and pay for your graduate school.

Then, if you are also willing to work and work hard at dreary jobs, willing, in fact, to suffer boredom and abuse, and slog ahead, and show some brains and some talent, they like that and will reward that. To certain limits. To certain levels. To the level just below them.

The banking world is full of stories about people with the wrong names, religions, backgrounds who got their law degrees at night, who were financial wizards, who were acknowledged as the best in the business in trusts, or investments, or whatever, and who made it all the way up to executive vice-president, and whom everyone in the business knew were the best possible choices to be president, but who somehow always got passed over for that last leap up to that highest level. Nobody knew the exact reason why because it is the Board of Directors of the bank that decides who will be the president of their bank, and nobody knows exactly why or exactly how they select one man over another. They certainly don't have to explain their actions to anyone, and they certainly don't violate the secrecy and sanctity of the boardroom.

Still, below the highest sacred level, things are infinitely better than they were just ten years ago. And then, of course, if you are a WASP and want desperately to make it in the garment business, I guess you have a few problems yourself. The world, as I was always taught, is not fair, but that's no reason not to try to conquer it.

Bankers and their deepest prejudices

Bankers, like other human beings, have prejudices. Most of the time, you probably don't worry about the inner hatreds of those other human beings because they don't directly affect you. Bankers are different.

As we all have seen, and the law has recognized in recent years, the prejudices of bankers can directly affect the way you live. If the loan officer has it in his mind that women are not "dependable" when it comes to money, he might turn down the loan application of a woman, ignoring the facts of the woman's case.

If the mortgage officer doesn't trust blacks and Hispanics, basically thinks they're all savages who periodically burn down their own neighborhoods when they're not out mugging and killing, he's going to "redline" that district—draw an imaginary red line around that area to mark it out-of-bounds for mortgages. If you happen to be black or Hispanic and you're applying for a mortgage loan, he'll lie to you, tell you "mortgage money is so tight these days..." If you happen to be white and you're applying for that same mortgage loan in that same "redlined" district, he might ask you if you've really looked hard at the neighborhood, walked around it, or he might simply write you off as unstable.

As we saw in earlier chapters, there are laws these days to prevent such discrimination. And banks take them seriously. Still, as I said, bankers are human. It's worth looking at the prevailing prejudices among bankers, understanding how they can come into play and affect the way a bank deals with you.

1. *"Watch out . . . he's Jewish, you know."* One of the great ironic lines in the entire history of banking is "The Jews own all the banks."

Excluding the Rothschilds, the single international exception, the only banks Jews own, or even serve as presidents of, are banks in Israel and a handful of small banks sprinkled here and there.

When I got out of college and started with The Bank of New York in 1965, one of the first things I noticed in the mean game of climbing the corporate bank ladder was that Jews didn't stand a chance. I had my own problems, coming from a frowned-upon minority, but my invisible obstacles were little compared with those of Jews. That was true throughout the banking world, and though conditions are somewhat better today, I would never advise a young Jewish man or woman fresh out of college to go into banking.

Though most of this prejudice was played out in somewhat muted ways, there were times when it was unbelievably blatant.

At lunch, it was common to hear a colleague talk about "a damn Jew" who was giving him a hard time over his account. Or, "the lousy kike doesn't know a good deal when he sees it."

Usually, such sweet remarks were not uttered if any of the few Jewish employees of the bank were around. Though I do remember once a young Jewish fellow, Peter, came to me trembling with rage because his boss hadn't been able quite to control himself. The boss basically hated everyone, but Jews were a special *bête noir*. On a pending loan arrangement, bossman had said to Peter: "Goddamn it, Peter, watch yourself or this lousy kike is going to try and take us again . . ."

When Peter walked over to my desk, he could barely speak. He was so outraged at his boss and equally angry with himself for not having said anything to the awful man. Peter left the bank not long after.

All of this anti-Semitism, it is important for you to understand, is always tempered by bottom-line reality. Neither Peter's boss, nor any lesser anti-Semite, was going to let his feelings stand in the way of doing business with those dreadful Jews. We wanted their business, just as we wanted the business of everyone else, including blacks, women, Hispanics, Indians, hermaphrodites, anyone with money.

But there was a difference. You were supposed to approach Jews in business deals with a special wariness. "They're a Jewish law firm, you know. . . ." and the rest was left unstated. You were supposed to understand. "Well, he's Jewish . . . uh . . ."

I recall one major effort we made to get the banking business of one of the most successful stockbrokers and investment bankers in New York, Mr. N., who was also a prominent Jew.

He had two accounts with us, small for him, about $100,000 in their balances, and we wanted his real business in the worst way. If we could attract the bulk of his banking, we might then lure some of his partners, and they might bring in some of their big clients, and that is what is known as striking gold in the banking business.

Mr. N., as you might imagine, was no fool. He knew we wanted him, and there was something he wanted from us. He wanted us to lend $1.5 million to a real estate development corporation he was involved in. Sadly, it was not the best of times for real estate, but the possibility of landing Mr. N. and his associates meant we had to avidly pursue him and the deal.

My associate worked out our general strategy. He harbored two particular concerns. "I want that business, John," he said, "crazy not to. But we've got to be extremely careful. We're not doing any real estate financing these days, as you know, so we've got to be extremely circumspect there." He paused and shook his head. "The other thing, you've got to watch out. He's Jewish, and a notorious horse trader, know what I mean . . ."

Caveats or not, we went after Mr. N. as hard as we could. Lunches at the bank, at my associate's club, dinners, meetings in Mr. N.'s office.

In the end, the whole thing came apart, not for any prejudicial reasons but because the deal, finally, was a bad one for us for a number of solid banking reasons.

I'm sure Mr. N. knew what kind of deal it was too and probably figured he had nothing to lose by trying, using the attraction of his potential business as bait. We were all playing the same game, as often happens in banking.

I don't know what actually happened to that deal, probably he got the loan, but from a much less conservative bank than ours. That's another matter. That's a clean business decision. The old bottom line.

2. *Blacks and Hispanics.* Blacks and Hispanics really did not exist in the banking world. Until recently, they were not hired, and their business was so limited, anything above the level of the most modest Special Checking Account from some clerical worker was a real exception.

I recall a few occasions when black businessmen sat at my desk on the platform, discussing their business and banking affairs, raising questions about loans and interest, just like any small businessman would.

But I also recall that when each of those black men left my desk, someone came over and asked me, "What the hell was that all about?" They were especially concerned by one black man with a shaved head, leather vest, jeans, and boots, whom they assumed was in the heroin business.

Once again it was a combination of the law and the bottom line that altered matters. Ethnic banks developed, and the largest banks in cities all over America opened new branches in black and Hispanic areas to cater to that business.

As a bank with limited branches to start with, we never expanded that way. And while I found a bit more business in the 1970s coming from black businesses, it was still small and, internally, still looked at with suspicion.

Interestingly, as we consider racial prejudice, I never found any toward Orientals in the bank. These days, of course, bankers look on all Japanese businessmen as geniuses. But going back a bit, it was the Chinese who were given special respect.

At one point, our bank had two of six senior vice-presidents who were Chinese. Both were brilliant, and needless to say, without a trace of an accent.

3. Gays, or "committed bachelors."

Looking back, I have to say that there have been officers of our bank who were what I could reasonably call "screaming queens." The senior officers of the bank simply chose not to notice. Instead, these people were spoken of as "committed bachelors."

They were largely in positions in which they dealt with older women, and everyone marveled at the way this one or that one handled the women so smoothly, with such natural rapport and style. No one ever whispered the word homosexual.

There were other, less obvious homosexuals I knew, who kept their private lives very private. And with very rare exceptions, I think that would be unchanged in the banking world today.

4. Rich women and all the others. The prejudicial treatment of women by banks has a special history.

There has always been one kind of woman cherished by banks, rich ones. But they were always rich by accident of birth or by virtue of a husband's wealth, so their cases have little bearing on the broader attitudes of bankers toward the majority of women.

Rich women were always coddled, usually by elderly women employees of the bank. Anyone named Mrs. Vanderbilt, it was assumed, wanted to sit and have tea with our mature Miss Austin in our special sitting room. There, in quiet and privacy, they could discuss any questions Mrs. Vanderbilt might have regarding her accounts. In fact, it was rare that a Mrs. Vanderbilt herself came into the bank. She had scores of advisers, lawyers, male family friends to handle all that mystifying money magic. But when she and her ilk did come,

they most likely came to something like The Fifth
Avenue Bank, an independent bank specializing in wealthy
women, mostly widows. Most conveniently located at
Fifth Avenue and Forty-fourth Street, it had a spacious
stable attached where madame's carriage could be parked,
while madame was having her tea and money chat next
door. If the wind blew in the wrong direction, well,
madame and everyone else would simply ignore the
barnyard smells that wafted through the bank.

The Bank of New York bought The Fifth Avenue
Bank in 1948, and though the stable is gone, those
precious gray-haired widows still have their tea and talk
in the surroundings to which they have been eternally
accustomed. (We also make house calls on such ladies,
but more on that, later.)

As for the rest of the women in the world, banks
thought very little of them, and badly at that.

In the 1950s and 1960s when I was starting out, it
was apparent to me that women were dismissed in
banks everywhere, not to be taken seriously as employees,
or customers.

The average banker began by assuming that a woman
was supposed to be at home. If that were so, a serious
job for her was out of the question. Maybe a part-time
thing, but surely nothing like a dedicated career.

That meant she had no real place as an employee of
the bank, or as a good loan customer.

If she had a full-time job, he further assumed, something was wrong with her. She couldn't accept her role
in life, was out to prove something strange. And who
needs that?

Or, maybe she isn't married, yet, so she's coming to
the bank for a job. But we all know that's only until she
meets the right man, hopefully in the bank, some
stable, perhaps even privately wealthy banker.

If a single woman with a job came into the bank for a
loan, the loan officer would dismiss the job as some
temporary fling, something so she can be closer to the
stores she likes to shop in.

If the woman was a working mother, even worse.

How long can she possibly keep that job? he asked himself. She's going to have to give it up to take care of that kid.

If she were divorced, he instinctively sided with the absent husband, who probably had to pay too much in alimony. The banker in him added: He'll wise up, figure a way to cut back on that, so this figure she's got down here for alimony, which is supposed to show me that she has enough coming in to pay back the loan, that's a phantom. I certainly can't place any value on that. That's not like salary or dividends that she's earning. And if she remarries, the alimony will stop altogether.

When it came to hiring women, banks maintained that women weren't very smart. Not at money. Couldn't be, not according to the preconceptions stated above. Women didn't have the strength men have, nor the ability to see through all those so-called complicated financial issues of banking.

Furthermore, it was ridiculous to imagine that a woman could possibly have the guts to negotiate the best deal. They could be beaten by any man. All he'd have to do is raise his voice, and the stupid bitch would collapse in tears.

Beyond that, a lot of the banking business is done over a bottle of whiskey. We entertain a lot, conduct some of our biggest business that way. Women can't even enter some of our best clubs, for goodness sake. And how in the world is a woman going to take some of these customers out on the town, get them drunk, and get them laid? Ridiculous. Obviously, she can't do any of those key things, so she obviously couldn't handle a key job in the bank.

Attitudes change slowly. Women know that such blindness was hardly limited to bankers. They encountered the same prejudice and duplicity in every business.

I don't believe that the attitudes have changed all that much among bankers or businessmen at large. But the law has.

There are federal and state laws that require banks to have a percentage of their staff on the management level be female. Which means we now must not only hire females, but the laws have forced us to rethink how we're going to use them. It's not enough to dump them in the traditional places because the law says it's not enough. Can't get away with making them all tellers, or administrative assistants, or even so-called assistant treasurers in charge of tea and rich widows.

That was the first general response among banks to the federal equal hiring laws. Make them assistant secretaries, let them review computer printouts. But the feds said no, give them real jobs with positions equal to those you give men.

The changes were made with great reluctance, some overt, some covert. Women were allowed for the first time to deal with commercial loans, for example. But I can recall countless times at the beginning of this great revolution when my boss would say, "I'm not sure we ought to give this one to Doris, John. Somehow I think Joe could handle this one a little better..."

The residual prejudices also affected promotions for women.

In a bank, there are basically two kinds of promotions. The first relates to title and salary. You move up from assistant vice-president to vice-president to senior vice-president to executive vice-president. The title improves each time, and so does your salary.

The other category is less public, yet more significant. It relates to increased responsibility and power. You can receive a better title and more money, but not be given much more responsibility and no more power.

Power and responsibility are what matter. They are in fact what most people who are serious about their careers in banking care most about, the power to affect the management and policies of the bank. And here, women are still shunted aside. Give them a few titles, let them be visible certainly on the floor, but when it comes to deciding whether the bank will go after foreign business, or expand by taking over smaller banks, or get in or out of the home mortgage business, the old boys' syndrome still prevails.

Women are made branch managers these days, which was totally inconceivable a few years ago. But those branches will be very special. Generally, it is the Upper East Side branches in New York, boutique operations, whose clientele are largely, once again, little, old rich women from the East Side. You rarely see women running the branches for any bank in the busiest mid-town areas, or the flagship branches in the heart of any downtown business district.

And, I doubt that you will see many in my lifetime.

Banking is not a business I would recommend to any smart female MBA, or woman fresh out of law school. Not yet. My daughter is sixteen years old. Maybe by the time she's finished with school, banking—business at large, indeed the world at large—will have truly changed in its roots, and at the top.

The power of the bottom line to effect change

When it comes to women as customers these days, once again the bottom line applies. Banks want good business, period. If your money is green, we want your account.

In the 1960s and 1970s, as more and more women were getting better jobs, earning bigger salaries, starting their own businesses, it became obvious to bankers that this was a substantial new consumer market.

I was a loan officer during much of that period, and I could see things changing. No matter what preconceptions a loan officer might have held, when a woman came in to see him and she was earning, in those days, $20,000 to $30,000, he had to look closely at the evidence. That was more than he was earning.

My own experiences with commercial loans from

women who were starting their own businesses might tell you something.

I remember a woman who had started her own advertising agency and had come to us for a loan so she could expand.

At our first meeting, I flirted with her. Outrageous, I know, but she was an attractive woman, and unthinkable as it is; our first conversation started out in a very unbusinesslike way. Nothing scandalous. We were, after all, sitting there in the middle of the main floor in our Fifth Avenue branch in plain view of dozens of customers, not to mention my very proper branch manager boss. But there was banter, some small talk, much more eye contact than I had ever known before with any other small businessperson who had come to my desk to borrow money. Freud maintained there is no such thing as a Platonic relationship between a man and a woman, that the sexual element is always there, even if deeply buried. Dealing with my first women "small businessmen" proved the theory.

We got over the charm and the eye stuff and on to the real business, and I quickly found myself dealing with a situation that was widespread at that time.

The woman had made a very nice start, billed substantially in her first two years. She had been a copy writer, then creative director for a large New York agency before going on her own. I had seen her ads on TV, which helped, and could see from her books and contracts that she had a real business going. But I could also see, after half an hour of talking with her, that she didn't know much about running her business, or fully appreciate what can happen if you expand unwisely.

Most small businesses fail in the first three years because they have never planned or arranged for enough capital. They don't give themselves any margin, just in case business doesn't boom the way they pray it will. It almost never does. If it's going to work at all, it builds slowly. And then somewhere around the middle of the second year, when the thing is starting to take hold, it collapses because the brave entrepreneur has been foolish, uninformed, or misinformed. He or she has no more capital, just when it is needed most, for that last haul.

The other most common financial problem with small businesses is success. If they do manage to get out of the woods, again usually after three years of perilous struggle, they don't know how to grow. Their eyes see only stars, and suddenly that modest woman's clothing store is going to become Neiman-Marcus overnight. Or, the specialty food store is going to license franchises, all over America, all over the Universe, become Coca-Cola and McDonald's rolled into one.

The advertising woman was clearly going to survive the critical three-year period. But her plans for expansion beyond that were unbelievably grandiose, based largely on her belief that she could get this account and that account on nothing more than a glimmer of a chance.

Also, her grasp of some business fundamentals was loose. Cash flow, for example, is not very complicated, but no one succeeds at business without understanding and controlling it. It means just what it suggests, how the cash actually flows into and out of your business. I could see that several of her clients were very slow in paying her. But in her mind, when she billed a client, she had that money.

In fact, no one defaulted. But it makes an enormous difference to your business if you have to wait three months before you have the cash in your account. It means among other things that whatever you were planning to do with that money has to be delayed, or you have to borrow the money yourself if you don't want to wait. Borrow and pay the interest, of course, an additional cost of doing business.

She wanted to borrow $50,000 from us. I saw promise in her as a customer, especially if I could get her to bring in someone—male or female—who could guide her through some of the business operations that were foreign to her.

That was the key to it. Her problem was not that she was a woman. Her problem was that she was new to business.

It could be argued of course that one causes the other, that because she was a woman, she had been deprived of the opportunity to get business experience. The same argument is used with other minorities when it comes to bank loans, or hiring, or education.

But my concern was lending $50,000 to someone who was new to business and deciding what the bank's risk would be. I would have had exactly the same concerns if a male with a new ad agency came to me for a $50,000 loan to expand it.

On the basis of the numbers and facts of business life, I could have turned this woman down. And I know that a number of my colleagues did, under similar circumstances. No question, in those decisions, the old clichés about women not being dependable when it came to money tipped the scales in their minds.

I got her the loan. Not because I was such a wonderful person, or because I was the first male on the block to have my consciousness raised. But because I was always looking to make loans where I thought everything was going to turn out okay for the bank. That was my job. The more good loans I showed on my record, the more I would be paid and promoted.

With women, at that time, I had to wage a special educational campaign with one of my bosses. He didn't trust women, of course. He also hated Jews and blacks, while Hispanics were beneath his raging contempt.

So I continually kept dropping sly comments on his head. "Fascinating story in the *Times* today about women making more than $50,000 a year . . ." "I've got an awfully promising new prospect. A Preferred Customer for over five years, nice, middle-five figure balances in the company account, business booming, needs $100,000 for expansion," I'd say, and after his eyes lit up, I'd add: "Very bright woman . . ."

The climate changed for women in banks as it changed

for women outside of banks. Modest efforts by men like myself didn't matter nearly so much as the facts of the marketplace.

Before long, our bank and practically every large bank in the country began special marketing approaches to attract women, making particular use of financial seminars.

They were all run by women bankers, of course, and the advice was exactly the same as any banker would give to a man or a woman, who was beginning to make good money for the first time. But the subliminal message was the same: "This is catch-up ball we're playing because, of course, we were never allowed to learn about money; that was all left to the men. Well, we're all in this together, now, and believe us, you can do it. You really can. I did it. Look how well I did it. I'm a vice-president of this great big bank. I learned and so can you. You've never had to balance your checkbook before or manage a cash flow, or understand the secrets of an investment portfolio. Now you do, and you will, believe me."

I attended a number of those seminars, as the token male. Though I didn't do much more than smile and nod and answer the occasional question, the bank wanted me there because we didn't want to overdo the business of separate and newly equal. This was not the formation of a women's club within the bank, we wanted to say. Also, we knew that any reasonably sophisticated woman knew that our bank was not all women, that it was in fact, mostly men.

What struck me was that the advice our women VP's were giving was the same advice our mature assistant secretaries used to give over tea, tête-à-tête, to the Mrs. Vanderbilts. But of course, the great difference here was that nobody in that seminar had ever even met a Vanderbilt.

How to fight back, if they discriminate against you

The combination of bottom line and The Equal Credit Opportunity Act is powerful. I can assure you that no banker wants to bring a government inspector, never mind a lawsuit, down on his house. The fear of fines and publicity is by now part of a banker's radar.

Still, you might encounter a loan officer on a bad day who can't control his prejudice, and his irrational attitude might cost you a loan.

You can defend yourself, and the first step in your battle plan is to decide whether you want to win a war or a battle.

If you have been turned down for a loan, and you feel your earnings, credit, numbers in general, merited the loan, so the only reason for the rejection is that you are a woman, a black, or some other minority, you can make a federal case of it.

You can write to the Board of Governors of the Federal Reserve System in Washington; you can go directly to the attorney general's office in your state or one of the other government agencies listed in the appendix of this book, and you can blanket the bank with carbons of all your angry letters.

That is what I call trying to win a war. It will be a tough, extended fight, and you had better be absolutely certain of your case before starting it. Unless you are right, the bank will fight back as hard as it can. In the end, of course, you might win, and not only will your particular bank be chastened (and fined), but your triumph will send shock waves throughout the banking world. You will have made it easier for other women, blacks, etc., to get loans.

As valiant as this might be, I don't recommend it. My advice is to try and win the battle, your personal battle.

First, be sure of what has really happened. Maybe you felt the loan officer was condescending, even a bit dismissive. Let's assume you are a woman and you heard him make a questionable remark, something about "the salaries being paid to girls in business these days." Maybe you're right and he is prejudiced against women.

But what about your case, completely apart from that? You saw earlier in the book how a bank weighs the elements on your loan application. Exactly how is your credit profile? Do you, in fact, show a history of delinquent accounts? Or, are you now carrying other, heavy debts? New to your job?

In other words, try to be dispassionate about your financial condition. Maybe the reason for your loan rejection is right there in the numbers, and the loan officer's attitudes have nothing to do with it.

If, however, you satisfy yourself that you should have gotten the loan, that your numbers and statistics hold up, at least put you in a gray category, then get out your stationery.

Write the first letter to the branch manager. Remember who and what he is likely to be. Don't make him angry, make him concerned. Do not sound shrill or overtly threatening, and above all, do not beat a loud ideological drum.

"I could, of course, be mistaken, and forgive me if I am, Mr. Bigelow, but I would ask you to look at the facts..." you tell him, calmly, and spell out your data. "Nevertheless, despite what would seem to me sufficient support for the loan, I was rejected.

"I was surprised by the result, and on consideration, I must confess that I had the feeling that the man I was dealing with, Mr. Connell, viewed my application in a less than even-handed manner, simply because it was coming from a woman.

"As I said, perhaps I am mistaken, but I would very much appreciate your reviewing the whole situation, and after you have done so, if you feel that it would be worthwhile, I could discuss a new loan situation with a different loan officer..."

When Bigelow gets a letter like that from you, he's going to want to do something, fast. From the tone of the letter, he assumes you are a reasonable woman, and a reasonable woman might just have a reasonable cause to complain. He also knows that prejudice among his bank officers exists. Maybe with Connell, he knows it is a problem. Perhaps yours is not the only complaining letter of this sort he's received about Connell.

Most of all, he's not going to endanger his own record by allowing this to balloon into a lawsuit for the bank.

He'll take the letter directly to Connell's desk and rub his nose in it. "What's going on here?" he'll say, trying to catch Connell off guard. And he'll watch Connell's response very carefully. If he senses that in fact Connell was unfair to you, he'll make life miserable for Connell and pleasant for you.

He'll phone you and be full of qualified apologies. He knows he's juggling dynamite, and he'll be so careful with his words, so circumspect, you might not be sure at first what he's saying. "Perhaps, as you suggest in your letter, Miss Armstrong, there was something a bit astray, here. I've had a thorough discussion with Mr. Connell—one of our best people, Miss Armstrong—and he was deeply disturbed at the very suggestion that he might have been in any conceivable way less than proper and professional in handling your application. Nevertheless, lest there be a shred of such concern on your part, I would like you to come in, any time at your convenience, and let me introduce you to Mrs. Walton. Mrs. Walton is one of our senior loan officers, and she would be happy to review your problem with you, and handle a new loan application for you . . ."

If you were right to start with, and there was some discrimination, you can be sure that this time around, gray area or not, you'll get the loan.

If you were wrong to start with, don't expect the bank to run from a fight.

If Bigelow confronts Connell with your letter and Connell tells him that your credit report was bad, or he had to call you on several overdrafts over the last couple of years, or any number of other legitimate reasons for not lending you money, Bigelow will listen very closely to his man. And he might very well decide that Connell is right. In which case, he will tell him to pull together every piece of documentation against you he can find.

Connell will go into the files, find any Call Reports or other meeting memos he or anyone else at the bank filed after having some sort of meeting with you. If he doesn't find anything useful, he might just make one up for his file. I've heard of that being done.

There might actually be the stuff he's looking for, a comment a while back that you couldn't be reached when there was some trouble with your account. Other signals that you are not very businesslike in your affairs with the bank.

Connell might make a credit check of his own on you, calling a few of the stores you charge at, chatting with their credit managers.

Meanwhile, Bigelow will make his call to you, and while being just as polite as possible, he will tell you, in very careful terms, that unfortunately, after reviewing your situation with Mr. Connell, the bank feels that there was nothing untoward or unfair involved in your treatment. "I can assure you, Miss Armstrong, though this will not be much comfort to you, but still, let me assure you that your loan application was turned down for traditional banking reasons only . . ." He'll tell you what they were and encourage you to try again in a few months.

You might not like Bigelow's rounded little speech, but control yourself. Do not, above all things, threaten him and the bank. When a banker, especially a banker who has reason to believe he's in the right, hears blackmail, the loss of his job, threats of lawsuits, terrible publicity, trouble through political friends in high places—when he hears that, his back goes up. Bigelow will remain formally pleasant with you, but he won't give an inch. "I'm sorry to hear you talk that way, Miss Armstrong, but I'm afraid there's nothing I can do. You simply do not qualify for that loan . . ."

If you remain unconvinced and still think you have been wronged by the bank, write another letter. This time to the president of the bank.

Once again, tone is everything. If you cannot conceal your outrage, you can be sure the president is going to sigh, "Not another one," and bounce your letter back to Bigelow. His note attached will read: "Get rid of this."

There is always the chance that the president has recently suffered a visit from an examiner from the state banking commission, investigating a similar charge. Bank presidents don't like to be subjected to the questions and skepticism of low-paid state employees. Your bank president might receive your letter, your lucid and calm letter, and he might sigh in a different way. His note to Bigelow under these circumstances would be: "Give her more attention."

But chances are, if Bigelow is prepared to defend the bank's good name and is armed with a substantial file from Connell and solid prudent banking reasons for denying you the loan, then the president will listen to him, not you. And in that case, you can complain to the appropriate government agencies, and if you still don't get satisfaction, it will be your lawyers against the bank's.

Going to court against a bank is not the best of moves. Such a suit can be eternally long and expensive, and chances are the bank has more money than you. Further, the bank wouldn't let matters go to court, unless it was extremely sure of its case.

But that is a bleak scenario, caused only by your own misjudgment of yourself as a loan candidate. If, however, your judgment is accurate and you have cause to complain about discrimination, do it in the genteel style that will win them over to your cause. No matter how angry you are, how much you want to throttle them. Play the game their way, and you will win. I have seen it work.

Chapter 13

God bless the Mrs. Aspinwalls of this world

It was the nicest apartment I had ever been in. On Fifth Avenue, of course, ten rooms in the Seventies, even the elevator with its burnished mahogany paneling and its white-gloved operator spoke of money, old money.

Every other week, I would ride up that elevator to have martinis at four with a woman I will call Mrs. Aspinwall.

Mrs. Aspinwall was a short, slight, almost birdlike woman, with trim gray hair and sharp brown eyes. At seventy-eight, she had been widowed for twenty years, and I wanted her money. For the bank, of course, but still I wanted it, and those sharp eyes reminded me every other Wednesday that I had better step carefully, she was protecting her own nest.

To be exact, I should say I wanted more of her money. She was worth about $12 million, and we already had some $4 million of that in the form of stocks and bonds sitting in our vaults in what is called a Straight Custodian Account.

Having $4 million in the vault is better than not having $4 million in the vault, but basically all we were doing with that $4 million was keeping it safe. That's what a Straight Custodian Account is: keep the certificates safe, send Mrs. Aspinwall a monthly statement that tells her what's gone up, what's gone down, what her dividends are.

For that, we collect a small fee, on $4 million it was about $4,000 a year. Not much compared to what we might earn if we could convince Mrs. Aspinwall to let us *manage* those stocks and bonds, move them and perhaps some other investments she had into a portfolio that we would manage, buying and selling in the marketplace for her instead of letting the stuff sit and collect vault dust.

I suggested that the $4 million was better than nothing. In fact, it was considerably better because it gave the bank and me some kind of relationship with her, some excuse to be in touch with her. It was my job to use that excuse to develop a much fuller relationship. Not only did we want to manage her portfolio, we also wanted to be named by her as trustee and executor of her will.

That's a good business, being executor of a will, especially if there is a lot of money in the estate and the whole thing is not too complicated. Individual states set the fees that executors may collect for their services. In New York, there's a sliding scale going from 5 percent of the first $100,000 of the estate down to 2 percent of everything over $5,000,000. For Mrs. Aspinwall and her $12 million, we could collect about $275,000 to do the job, which could be a very simple one for us.

As a twenty-seven-year-old junior officer in the Trust Department, there was nothing more important to my job and my future with the bank than making martinis at four for Mrs. Aspinwall.

Being a woman with a good sense of herself and what

she liked, she knew exactly how she wished those martinis. None of that gin and vermouth sloshed together in a glass. Mrs. Aspinwall wanted seven parts gin to one part vermouth, exactly, carefully mixed in a silver shaker and poured into well-frosted, long-stemmed glasses. Her husband had taught her, a long time ago.

Her husband had been a businessman in New York and had built quite successfully upon the money they both had inherited. He had left Mrs. Aspinwall with her Fifth Avenue apartment, one of the largest houses in East Hampton, an estate in Hobe Sound, and her entire investment portfolio.

They had been married for thirty years, and though they had no children, theirs seemed like a marriage full of love. Ironically, that was one of Mrs. Aspinwall's problems. Her feelings for her late husband were so deep that she didn't want to touch anything he had done. If he had bought those stocks and bonds, they were good enough for her. In fact, he had been an intelligent, if conservative, investor, so her money was fairly secure. But times and companies do change. I remember hearing a dreadfully cute analogy another trust officer had created for one of his little old ladies: "Portfolios are like gardens, you see. If they aren't tended and weeded, they wither and die."

I could not bring myself to play the friendly gardener, but Mrs. Aspinwall did have a problem. Someone should have been reviewing and adapting her holdings to the times.

Her other problem was very common among widows like her. They had never done anything connected with their estates, except to sign on dotted lines as instructed by attorneys. In those days, their husbands were responsible for everything financial. Now, alone, they were scared and ignorant, a tough combination.

It was a combination that made so many of them such easy marks for unscrupulous lawyers and hustler brokers. To be sure, there I was courting a seventy-eight-year-old widow to get her business for the bank. But, believe me, there's a great difference between us and those

lawyers and brokers. You can argue over whether our
bank or banks in general produce good enough returns
on portfolios. Maybe we tend to be too conservative.
But we don't steal from widows and orphans, and we
don't play fast and loose with their wealth. When
another widow, Mrs. Woods, came to me, sent to me
one day by a friend of hers who was worried about her,
it was too late. A hotshot broker had taken her $3 million
estate and blown it apart. All those go-go growth stocks
in the 1960s that couldn't miss had somehow missed.
She was left with $200,000 which was better than
nothing; but it was $2,800,000 less than she'd had three
years before.

So, there was a nice civil side to my Wednesday
afternoons with Mrs. Aspinwall. Not to confuse me with
her minister. There was nothing charitable or Christian
in my good deed. It was business. But I was a relatively
honest businessman, and I could provide some services
for Mrs. Aspinwall that would really benefit her.

If she could trust me, that is. Before she'd take the
services from me, she had to get to like me and trust
me, and that was why she had invited me to her
apartment. For months before, I had been phoning her
on the slightest pretext, even sending her flowers on
the anniversary of her account with us.

When she was sailing to Europe on a two-month trip,
she had called the day before to ask me if I thought she
might need a letter of credit. I got it immediately and
showed up with it, a bottle of champagne, and my wife
the next day at her stateroom on the *Queen Mary*.

It was after that trip in fact that she called one day,
said she had a few questions, and wondered if I might
come up to her apartment. "I don't like banks, John,
going into them—if you know what I mean?"

We sat and sipped our perfectly frosted martinis in
the living room, a salon full of large overstuffed chairs
and sofas, the austere portrait of Mr. Aspinwall's grand-
father on one wall, a few lighter still lifes and a land-
scape on another. A grand piano, its shiny top covered
with silver-framed photos filled one corner of the room.

Under the piano, everywhere it seemed, there were Persian rugs, faded, delicate beauties.

I preferred the Queen Anne chair at the far end of the room. I could really sink into it, and from there I could watch Mrs. Aspinwall on the pale blue sofa and, in the other direction, gaze out on Central Park and a great swath of the New York skyline. It was a spectacular view from the sixteenth floor, wonderfully high over everything, above sounds. Being so high up with all those cushions and rugs and the heavy muffling furniture, the room was possessed by silence. It is a kind of silence I was to learn that belongs to the very rich, a treasure they take as much for granted as the rest of us do soap.

It was not complicated stuff, Mrs. Aspinwall was asking. In fact, most of it was pretty simple. A question about signing a stock power bothered her. She was unsure of the monthly cash statement on her custodial account. Something she'd heard about interest rates. Perhaps checking out a piece of advice from a friend about estate planning.

In fact, I never thought she was really so much interested in the content of my answers as the form. She was feeling me out. She was on the verge, pushing herself to make some big financial decisions, and they unnerved her. Did I seem to know what I was talking about? Did I seem to be trustworthy? Was I the person who could really lead her through those decisions? Was I really capable of handling her affairs? She knew the bank was behind me, and it had been her bank since she married into it. In the institution, she had complete faith. But what about me?

Usually she had one or two banking questions to ask first, then we just chatted—about her dead husband, about her travels. Every now and then something would remind her of money. "They're selling land in Surrey, John, for what I think is really very little. Is that something I should consider?" she'd ask, and those eyes would get very bright.

Months went by, and we developed a relationship. I

was the dutiful nephew. Concerned and knowing in my banker's suit, I made her frosted martinis, answered any questions she had, and listened attentively to her stories, even if I had heard them before.

Needless to say, there wasn't a thing related to banking that I didn't do for her. Or, anything else for that matter: "Mrs. Aspinwall, I don't know if you'd be interested," I said to her one day on the phone, "but yesterday you mentioned the musical *Grease*. And I just thought you might enjoy seeing it. The bank is able to obtain a few seats..."

"Oh, John, aren't you thoughtful. But I'm told it's sold out for months and months."

It was, but I had badgered our Public Relations Department to get the tickets. "Mrs. Aspinwall, if you'd like to go tomorrow night, I have two nice seats I could send up to you by messenger."

She actually gasped. "John, could you really? Oh, my goodness... Well, yes, I would like that, very much. How can I ever thank you, John?..."

I certainly could have offered suggestions. But I was ever discreet, in fact so discreet that I began to wonder after six or seven months, if I wouldn't have to get a bit more forward. And then my break came.

It was about a year after I had started my martini seminars. Mrs. Aspinwall called me from her place in East Hampton. A minor banking matter, but in the course of our conversation she mentioned in passing that her lawyer was driving out from New York the following day on a trust matter.

I leapt. One of the transcendent spiritual missions of a trust officer in a bank is to get the Mrs. Aspinwalls of the world to the point where they automatically think of their banker in connection with anything financial, anything legal that relates to their estate. The catechism goes, "Lawyer... accountant... banker... lawyer... accountant... banker..."

My Mrs. Aspinwall was almost at that point, but she still needed a bit of prompting. "Mrs. Aspinwall, if he's going to be discussing something related to your estate, do you think I might be of any help?"

"Help, John?"

"In case there's any question that touches on our end of things, I'd be delighted to drive out with him if you think I might be able to help."

"John, I hate to ask you to come all the way out here . . ."

"Not at all, Mrs. Aspinwall. I'd enjoy it. Haven't been to East Hampton for a long time, anyway."

The next day, I drove out with her lawyer. He was a young fellow, only a few years older than I. The firm had been the firm her husband used, but the senior partner who had handled their affairs and had been the executor of their wills had died. Inheriting younger partners was another common fate of wealthy widows, and I could see quickly with this man that Mrs. Aspinwall had not been lucky in the draw. The man was a familiar WASPy type to me, the right clothes, the right accent. His passion in life appeared to be sailing. Incredibly to me, he seemed to resent Mrs. Aspinwall, as if she were wasting his time with her silly problems, keeping him from life's real stuff, which was sailing the Atlantic single-handed.

It was, in short, a very good thing for Mrs. Aspinwall as well as myself that I forced myself into that meeting. In addition to his indifference, the man didn't know what he was talking about.

I'm not a lawyer, but my work had steeped me in various aspects of the law as they affect trusts. That day we were to talk about setting up a new trust fund for Mrs. Aspinwall.

The fellow explained it to her all wrong. I was careful in the way I corrected him, continually cushioning my statements with genteel padding: "I wonder if perhaps what we're talking about here is . . . Perhaps I'm wrong on this point, Jim, but I thought the tax consequences were slightly different . . ."

Mrs. Aspinwall got the point. She said little, but

those brown eyes flickered back and forth, back and forth, and registered every thrust and parry.

And then at the end of the meeting, it came. "John, I have a special favor to ask of you."

"Certainly, Mrs. Aspinwall."

"John, you're so good when it comes to all these complicated things about estate planning. You understand it all and make it all so simple and clear, even to an old lady like me who never balanced a checkbook in her life."

I forced a proper little laugh. "Mrs. Aspinwall, I'll always take a compliment from you, but you don't give yourself credit."

She held up her palm. "I know what I'm talking about, John. You really have a gift," she said. "What I'd like to ask of you is if you could come back out here next week. You see, my friends and I play bridge every Tuesday. I've told them all about you and how intelligent and nice and polite I think you are, and I've also told them I think they're crazy not to do something about their own situations, you know, some estate planning the way you and I have been talking."

I felt suddenly cold. I could only nod.

"And what I'd like you to do, if you would, is to come out next Tuesday when they're all going to be here for our card game and talk to them. I think you could do them a world of good, John, I really do. Could you do that for me?"

How I did not faint at her feet, I do not know. I even managed to speak. "Mrs. Aspinwall, I'd be delighted," I said. I wished at the moment I were in a movie, so the screen could go dark, and we could cut to the next scene, me and a roomful of very rich little old ladies. I was afraid, if I stayed in Mrs. Aspinwall's house a moment longer, she would change her mind, or I would pass out.

In a way, it was like a movie. One of the great distant dreams of every banker is that a wealthy client will introduce him to a wealthy friend. To have Mrs. Aspinwall offer me her entire gang, five more wealthy widows like herself in one sitting, is a little like winning the singles, doubles, and mixed doubles titles at Wimbledon, your first time in the tournament. Not too common.

I would like now to be able to tell you about my triumph the following Tuesday in East Hampton, and how I won all of their hearts and accounts, and they lived happily ever after, and so did I because I became the youngest president The Bank of New York ever had. That's how it would have been in the movie. Life, alas, is different. But fear not. There is a fairly happy ending.

First, the following week's game was postponed. Illness. Then, as it happened, my breakthrough with Mrs. Aspinwall came at a time when I was being transferred out of the Trust Department to become a loan officer.

So I had to hand over Mrs. Aspinwall and her cronies to the fellow who replaced me. Yet, all was not lost. He did a nice job of following up. Mrs. Aspinwall did name the bank the manager of her portfolio as well as the trustee and executor of her will. In addition, two of her friends brought all their banking to us. And, I got full credit within the bank for the long, careful job I had done with Mrs. Aspinwall.

What was also nice was that from time to time she would insist on my handling matters for her, even though they were no longer part of my work. So when there was a problem with our correspondent bank, the one we had sent her to in Hobe Sound, I flew down and straightened it out for her. It could have been handled on the phone. But why pass up a few days in Hobe Sound in the winter? And why not give the most special of treatments to the dear Mrs. Aspinwalls of this world? They deserve it. Besides, I liked *my* Mrs. Aspinwall.

For obvious reasons, banks really like rich people, even if they're not aged widows.

To show our pleasure with them, we'll do practically

anything. I sent Mrs. Aspinwall flowers, tickets to the hottest Broadway show, champagne, and flew to Hobe Sound to iron out a little problem for her. That's only the frosting. As I'll explain later in this chapter, we have a large bag full of enticing goodies for them, like lending them money at lower interest rates than we lend it to you, large amounts of money with little or no collateral, or completely flexible payment schedules.

It's not just that we're a snobbish bunch. There are good business reasons for such favoritism. First, of course, the rich are where the money is, to paraphrase Willie Sutton. Not only do they offer us the opportunity to bring millions into our bank, but their potential is so heartwarming.

There is the chance that they will earn or inherit even more millions.

There is the chance, as with Mrs. Aspinwall, that they will send us their nice, clean, rich friends.

There is the chance for lots of business—good, safe loan business. What a pleasure it is to loan, say, $100,000 to someone named Belmont or Harriman or du Pont, especially when the nice fellow secures the loan, gives us over $100,000 in stocks for safekeeping. Especially when we've been doing business with that nice fellow for a while, know that he handles his affairs with some degree of responsibility, and is not the playboy black sheep of a distinguished flock.

Of course, the rich can be as imperfect as the rest of us, and it was my job as a loan officer to look beyond the fancy name and judge the individual, just as I was supposed to do with anyone, rich or otherwise, who asked us for a loan. In fact, a flawed richie can be a huge headache, or worse, for a bank, bigger than a flawed normal person since the numbers involved are usually so much bigger.

Typically, the richie comes to us as a young person. Many of them are born into banks, ones their families have been using, perhaps owning for generations. I get a call from his mother or father. "I want my son to try to learn to take care of his affairs..."

Not long ago, I was sent such an heir by the senior partner of an investment company. We handled all their family banking, as well as the firm's. I knew various members of the family, and I had even, some years before, set up a trust in Derek's name.

Still, I knew from the start, this kid would be trouble. We had an eleven A.M. meeting, for which he showed up at noon, fresh from his morning shower, not a hint of apology about him. He'd been out of school six years, had bounced among three different jobs—investing, selling real estate, and advertising.

Sure enough, after months of covering all of Derek's bad checks—one of the first of our special services for the select—I came back from lunch one afternoon and found two beefy men in bad suits sitting in one of our most finely appointed conference rooms.

"Who are those guys?" I asked the fellow at the desk next to mine.

"Cops," he told me.

"Cops?" I replied, incredulous. "Are you kidding? Have we been robbed?"

"Could be. They want to talk to you about wonder boy. Seems this time, he's done more than bounce checks."

In fact, he had been bouncing checks on accounts that had been closed, which is much worse than your garden-variety bounced check. Not only that, he was writing them all over the country, then using the money to buy drugs with forged prescriptions. The police could not locate him, but they could find his bank. They wanted a chat, which I and two others had with them. We did not tell them anything that violated Derek's privacy; we are extremely careful about that. These cops had no court order, they were simply investigating and searching. In fact, they knew more about Derek than we did.

The kid was an alcoholic, addicted to various drugs, and incapable of controlling his life in any way. Of course, with rich Mommy and Daddy always there, I guess he never felt he had to be responsible for his life in any way. Before long, he surfaced, and we were sending checks to various sanitoriums, very expensive drying-out spas and rehabilitation centers.

The rich have problems learning to live with their money just as the rest of us do. Only with them, the problems get fairly baroque, and often what they need is not a good banker but a good psychiatrist.

I inherited a case like that, a man I'll call Hubert, about sixty years old who was worth $3 million in stocks and investments, in addition to various family real estate holdings. He had never worked at a real job but was always dabbling at things, playing at the fringes of life. Twenty-five thousand into a small print gallery, $50,000 into a condo development project in Vail, Colorado, small pieces of Broadway shows. He made some money, lost some money, enjoyed himself, and didn't give anybody much trouble. Until now. When I inherited his case from another loan officer who was moving into another department, our bank was trying to collect $150,000 we had loaned to this man.

It was a "demand loan," so in theory, we could "demand" payment of the whole principal at any time. But in practice, as I've noted, that is rarely done. Our understanding with him was that he'd pay the principal back in two years and cover the interest with quarterly payments.

Our wealthy friend had taken his $150,000, and though he had now enjoyed our money for almost three years, he had not paid off a cent on the loan, and he was way, way behind on interest payments.

To be sure, he had secured the loan with stocks. But the last thing any bank wants is to "sell out" a millionaire customer, sell the stocks in order to get the loan money back. Messy, embarrassing for everyone, bad will all around.

So, another meeting was scheduled with the man to try once again to work things out, and that morning I reviewed his file.

Two things struck me.

First, we had lent him the money so he could buy a

boat. Not a boat he would then sail up to Newport, or down to Palm Beach, which, frivolous as it might sound, at least would be in character. No, this was a boat he was going to charter.

He was going into the boat-chartering business all by himself. There was nothing to indicate that he knew a thing about that business, which, as I've suggested, is one of the criteria we try to maintain on loans for new businesses. If you were to come in for a loan to start a new business, chances are pretty good that somewhere along the way I would probably ask you if by any chance you knew anything about the business you wanted to start with our money. Especially if you were not planning on bringing in any experienced partners. Not a word here about Hubert's experience in the boat-chartering business.

The second thing that caught my eye was that Hubert had been selling off an increasing amount of his stocks and bonds in recent months, presumably to pay a few of his bills elsewhere.

Those things troubled me, as I went into the conference room that afternoon and took my place with a few of my colleagues and Hubert at a glistening rosewood table.

We were all gentlemanly smiles, and Wilkens, the senior member of our little bank team, began by practically apologizing for having to bring Hubert back into this chamber yet again. "But, as you are undoubtedly aware, we have been discussing with you the problem on your demand loan, reviewing the matter for over a year now, and yet, to date, we have not received any payments from you, Mr. Hubert, not a penny toward the principal, and you have been continually delinquent in paying the interest." He spoke in the tone of a very understanding schoolmaster dealing with a troubled child. "And we thought that we should finally try to work something new out with you, Mr. Hubert. We are patient and understanding bankers, and we want to do everything we can to help. But we are still bankers, Mr. Hubert, and we have to try to be

businesslike, even with our favorite clients, like yourself..."

Whereupon, Mr. Hubert lifted his heavy body from
his large chair, walked to the far end of the room, and
proceeded to go round and round and round in a small
circle. He might have been doing a rain dance, though
at any minute I thought he was going to stamp his feet
and bawl.

Apparently, the others at the table had witnessed this
before because no one blinked, except me. They all
continued smiling, nodding, and Wilkens continued his
schoolmaster's homily.

Hubert suddenly stopped, pulled off his jacket, and
marched back to his chair. He said nothing, listening
with his head and eyes down, fiddling with the buttons
on his coat. Then he put it back on, and after he got it
just right, he rose again, marching to the end of the
room, and went into his circle dance.

After a few minutes, he took off his jacket again and
sat down in his chair. In two or three minutes, he was
sitting up, in preparation for another march and some
more circles.

He repeated this pattern over and over again throughout the meeting, which lasted forty-five minutes. We
did at least get him to speak—sometimes while he was
making his rounds, sometimes from his chair.

From what he replied to my question, it was clear
that among other things he suffered a common richie's
problem: Money was not very real to him. It was as if
we had given him $150,000 to buy a boat, and that was
nice because then, in addition to his assets of $3
million, he also possessed a neat boat worth $150,000.
He never faced the fact that he was supposed to pay
that loan off someday. After all, he had given the bank
more than $150,000 in his stocks, which in his mind
was as good as paying off the loan. Even better, because
in some magical way, he was eventually going to get
those stocks back from the bank, which meant that he
had increased his assets by $150,000.

He knew he had been a bad boy, but gee, certainly

we could understand better than anybody how tight money was these days, how the market was down and everything. My goodness, it wasn't as if he weren't good for it or wouldn't pay it back. Good Lord, it wasn't as if he were trying to cheat the bank out of anything. We certainly knew what he was worth, better than anybody.

A variation of that particular richie's disease goes like this: Since they know they're worth more than the loan, and they know you know, and we're all supposed to be gentlemen, and they're supposed to be getting some special treatment anyway, since, after all, they're not only giving you all their millions to handle, but so is their wife, so has their mother, their father, as well as *their* mothers and their fathers... how can anyone worry?

Nothing was really worked out except a new payment schedule, which I knew he would ignore because he was incapable of following it.

After the meeting, when he'd left the four of us sitting there, I asked at large: "How could we ever have gotten into this one?" I knew there was a possibility that Hubert had asked for his money at a time when the bank was extremely anxious to lend money and senior officers were applying terrific pressure on loan officers to make loans. During such sieges, obviously, standards are most flexible.

Or, perhaps the loan officer who had granted Hubert the money simply hadn't done his homework. He hadn't created any real profile of the man, which would be hard to avoid in Hubert's case. I would think that ten minutes with him and his rain dance would tell you something about lending him $150,000.

"How did we ever get into this one?"

Wilkens looked at me with surprise and a touch of scorn. "Get into it? Are you kidding, John? You see what the man's worth. His family has been banking with us since the flood."

"I don't care what he's worth. He's a loony, a certifiable loony. Don't we have a policy around here somewhere that says, 'No loans to loonies'?"

Wilkens brushed my remark away with a slow wave

of his hand. "C'mon," he said. "I just hope that maybe, now, we can get him to start paying."

One of the others spoke up cheerfully. "I don't think there's any doubt. That man got the message today."

"How would you like to make a little bet on that one?" I asked him. "Say $150,000? And I'd be willing to take it in the form of a yacht."

Five years later, the bank was forced to sell Hubert out, dump his stocks and bonds, and take our money.

Not that such an experience taught the bank anything. You might think that the lesson would have been, as I had suggested: Don't lend money to loonies. But bankers find it almost impossible to perceive the rich as loonies. Eccentrics, yes. Alcoholics, sometimes. Black sheep playboys, of course. But loonies? Loonies? No, loonies are poor folk. And for them, we certainly have a policy: Don't lend money to poor folks, especially if they're loonies.

You don't have to be born rich to be a Preferred Customer. Just so long as you have money.

We like lawyers a lot. They tend to keep good balances, recommend lots of their own clients to us, and often open Client Funds Accounts. These are temporary accounts for transactions where A makes a payment to B, and it has to be held until a contract is signed, or the like. So they put it in a Client Funds Account.

Same for accountants, who also send us new business. Investment counselors, money managers, other bankers are also on the preferred list.

Corporate executives, of all levels, get special treatment. We want their corporate business, and we never know which of today's assistant treasurers will become tomorrow's executive vice-president of General Motors.

The key with all these customers is "potential." Do we think the individual has potential to earn big bucks? Is the potential there for that person to send us other people?

Favored folk can vary from one part of the country to

another. In Iowa, good bankers know which farmers are to be on the Preferred Customer list, even if they come into the bank in overalls, smelling of horse manure. In Los Angeles, personal money managers and agents are extremely welcome. Think of all the rich clients they might represent, all those happy, mindless actors and actresses who bring in all those millions, even though they have real trouble adding and subtracting, and like, man, like wow, reading a monthly bank statement.

How banks perform for the rich, their Preferred Customers, is a model of an ideal world. Unfortunately, no bank can afford such personal attentiveness on a broad scale. Still, banks have evolved a number of special services from their experience with the wealthy and now offer these adaptations to average people in a variety of forms.

Let me pull together some seven categories of service we extend to rich folk, and then, in the next chapter, we can consider the adapted forms available to one and all.

No bounced checks

Chances are, if you write a check for more than you have in your account, you learn about it the painful way. The check bounces, and whether the error was innocent—you had subtracted wrong in your checkbook, or maybe your last deposit hadn't cleared fast enough—whatever the reason, you're faced then with the embarrassment, bother, even a petty fine from the bank to rub it in.

Not so for Preferred Customers. It is impossible for them to bounce a check.

If they make the same mistake as you, what we do with them is pay the check anyway. Then we give them a phone call, tell them that somehow this unthinkable thing has happened, probably because they're so busy they hadn't even realized what their balance was, or perhaps they had meant to write that check on one of their other accounts—we have a dozen stock excuses we make up for them. And then we ask them, if it's not too much trouble, to come down today, or send someone down to make a deposit to cover the check. Often, they do have other accounts with us, and we agree to make a transfer from one to the other, sparing them the tedious trip into the bank.

There are limits, of course. If I see a $20,000 overdraft, no matter whose account it is, I'm going to make a rather different phone call. Before committing the bank to an interest-free loan of $20,000, I'm going to satisfy myself that indeed we will be repaid that day.

Interestingly, all checks are treated equally by the system.

Every check that causes a Regular Checking Account to be overdrawn is flagged by the computer during the night, so that in the morning when I sit down at my desk, I have a list of all the accounts I'm responsible for that have been overdrawn, along with an Overdraft Record Card for each. Twenty, thirty, forty checks from my accounts are there on the list, with the amounts, the account numbers, names of the account.

With a glance at the list, I know immediately which accounts we're going to cover without any question. I can also see which ones are marginal, where I'd better make the phone call *before* we cover the check. I can also see, of course, all the rest, the ones we're going to let suffer.

The Overdraft Record Card, as you can see from the one here, gives me instant history. I can immediately see when the customer has overdrawn before, for how much, and what excuse he's offered. All of that is extremely important with people we don't know all that well or with anyone who is starting to show a pattern of overdrafts.

The computer prints out the same kind of list for overdrafts in Special Checking Accounts, but that's strictly for informational purposes.

No one with a Special Checking Account will be reprieved. We automatically bounce all those checks, usually little checks from little accounts, and automatically hit them with a service charge.

Though you might sweat and tremble with angst when you get one of those slips, in fact, your bank doesn't much care. Unless the amount of your bounced check is substantial, they really don't bother with it. It's your problem.

If you bounce checks habitually, however, especially if you've got Special Checking, then they do worry. That's one of the main reasons the computer bothers to print out a Special Checking list. Because if the bank officer who has general responsibility for your account sees that you keep bouncing them, he's going to give you a call, but his call will be a bit different from mine. He's going to tell you he's closing out your account. The bank doesn't want to do business with you. Go elsewhere.

And, in case you wonder, he does have every legal right to do that. As we saw, banks are tightly regulated by governmental agencies, and must adhere to various laws. But they remain private businesses, and they are no more required to do business with you than a restauranteur is required to serve you if he feels you're drunk and making too much noise in his establishment.

Preferred loan treatment

In Chapters 8 and 9, we followed you as you went after the $10,000 loan to redo your kitchen and bring new, long-awaited joy into your life.

The process would be different if you were one of our Preferred Customers. Then, you'd go into the bank and kind of hand the problem over to your banker. Here's what I need, you say. And he says, fine, let's see what the best way would be to give it to you. None of that stuff about loan applications and fearful TRW's and 20 percent–25 percent ratios.

							GROUP NUMBER	TOTAL NO. OF OVERDRAFTS	OVERDRAFT RECORD CARD	
ACCOUNT NO.				NAME					SIGN ONE – DO NOT INITIAL	
			OMIT PENNIES						PAY	DO NOT PAY
DATE	AVAILABLE FUNDS	UNCOLLECTED AMOUNT	AMOUNT FOR PAYMENT	AMT. AGAINST UNCOLLECTED FUNDS	OVERDRAFT AMOUNT	CAUSE, IF DETERMINABLE				
1.										
2.										
3.										
4.										
5.										
6.										
7.										
8.										
9.										
10.										
11.										
12.										
13.										
14.										
15.										
16.										
17.										
18.										
19.										
20.										

OTHER ACCOUNTS – CONTACTS – STANDING INSTRUCTIONS – ETC.

1-800-9982   RETURN THIS CARD BY 2 P. M. TODAY TO CREDIT DEPARTMENT.

Let's see what's best for you. Short term? Long term? Whatever you want. Perhaps you prefer a Demand Note? Pay us the $10,000 principal in, say, twenty-four months? You'd prefer thirty months? Sure, why not.

When it comes to interest, we also have special arrangements for our special people.

Our standard consumer loans, I explain to them, are going at 18 percent and yes, I agree with them, that is hideously high. But your business really matters to us, so why don't we give you this loan at half a point below the Prime Rate with a cap on it, so it can never go above 18 percent.

The preferred people, in other words, can get a whole variety of loans, all specially tailored to them, and they get them at lower interest rates than you have to pay.

Preferred folk also get the speediest of treatment from us. Sign here. Thank you. I'll have your account credited with $10,000 today.

No need to bother with a formal credit check. I know the person. I am familiar with the account. I've done the credit check in my own mind.

Investment advice and services

As we saw with Mrs. Aspinwall, we're always trying to convince the wealthy to let us manage their investment portfolios. But that's very big bucks. Most medium to large banks won't bother with your portfolio if it's worth less than $250,000. Smaller places take you on at $100,000.

On a lesser scale, if a Preferred Customer has an odd $10,000 to $15,000 sitting around and he's not sure what to do with it for the next several months, we figure it out with him. As we saw, it might be T-bills, or commercial paper, maybe a money market fund. We do it for them, and we don't charge them any service fees, either.

Free financial and estate planning

We're extremely happy to help our rich customers plan their estates, for obvious reasons. We insinuate ourselves, as much as we reasonably can, right into the middle of it. The more they turn to us for such guidance, the better.

But many Preferred Customers, for their own reasons, don't want us in the middle of their estates. They do want us, however, to help them with some early planning, to help them to understand some of the tax principles that are critical to any estate planning, to give them a general grasp of the problem areas they should start thinking about.

So they come to us for that and that alone. We give them extremely good advice, for nothing. Imagine what they might have to pay a tax lawyer for that time and advice. In fact, they usually do retain that tax lawyer, but later on, after they've gone through the basic course with us.

Introductions

If one of our Preferred Customers is going to Europe, we send letters ahead to banks so they will give our client the kind of treatment he is accustomed to receiving from us.

Or, perhaps one of them wants to buy a second home in the mountains, a weekend and summer place. If they want a mortgage from a local mountain bank, we make a call. I have done this a number of times, and the difference it makes is enormous.

We even help them locate their dream house. I had one client who decided she loved London so much and was spending so much time there that it would make sense to buy a place of her own. She had a mews house in mind.

I called the manager of our branch in London, and just as I expected, he was on top of the real estate market and also knew two or three dependable real estate brokers for her to use.

Similarly, if one of our special folk is actually moving away, we set him up with one of our correspondent banks in the new city. When that happens, we run the risk of course of having the correspondent bank woo our client away completely. Often, even if they move, they'll keep us as executor of their will, perhaps let us manage their portfolio as well. But it's a risk we're willing to take, one that frequently leads to splendid elbowing and slashing between us and the correspondent bank.

We also introduce our favorites to certain professionals. If they come to us saying they need a new lawyer or accountant, for example, we'll draw up a little list. Our practice is never to recommend only one. Then we're too responsible if things don't work out. But with a list, we can discuss the strengths and weaknesses of each, let them meet with each, and decide for themselves. No charge, of course, but a nice favor done for both the client and the lawyer or accountant. The client will certainly be grateful, if we are able to help him find, at long last, a lawyer he really likes and has confidence in. And that lawyer, as you can imagine, should be even more grateful at being sent, out of the blue, a millionaire. It is not surprising after such a mating that we find that lawyer sending us a client or two of his own who are dissatisfied with their present banks.

Genuine personal service

Here I'm not thinking of theater tickets and champagne. I mean real service. I mean when you've got a problem with your account, you are able to get it straightened out, quickly, cleanly, pleasantly. Service.

Let's say, it's a problem that goes back a few years. You need some checks you wrote then. You paid some bills, but now, after all this time, you get a letter from the collection department of that office equipment place saying you never paid them for their dictating machines. They've changed their record-keeping system, and they've made this discovery. You don't have the checks. You go to the bank and tell them, "I need copies of the checks."

If you're just another account, you explain your problem to some officer who doesn't know you. He says he'll do what he can do, please be patient because a search like that through all that microfilm takes time, but he'll do what he can.

He writes a memo to the operations department and weeks, months go by. Nothing. He doesn't know you, care about you, or want to be bothered with your problem. He's got other, much more important things to concern himself with.

However, when I have one of my special people come in with a problem like that, I call the head of the department in operations who's responsible for the microfilm. I explain the problem and make the point strongly that this is a very important customer of the bank.

In fact, he is unimpressed and unmoved. It's extra work, tedious work. But, he also knows that if he doesn't do something, since I'm making the effort to call him, I will get him in trouble with his boss.

In fact, I might just call his boss anyway, telling him that I have made this special request, and though I know how overburdened they are down there, I hope they can help me out.

When three days go by, I call the guy in operations again and nicely tell him that I've already had one chat with his boss, and we certainly do agree, this is a priority item. "It would certainly be to our mutual advantage, if we could help this customer out."

"I understand, Mr. Cook. We'll do the best we can." And I know that when he hangs up that phone, he will move my request out of pile B on his desk and into pile A, somewhere near the top.

Two days later, I'll have to call again, but by that afternoon, I can phone the client and say: "We've got it. It's on its way to you by messenger. I don't know what that company was trying to do to you, but you certainly paid them."

Without that kind of attention by me, without that kind of personal service, you could wait for weeks, for months, before you'd get your problem cleared up.

Wooing services

Some of these we glimpsed in my tale about Mrs. Aspinwall. Flowers and letters of credit, martinis at four, lunches at the bank to review matters, dinners at Four Seasons, whatever they like.

Whenever I took a client to an expensive lunch or dinner, I'd always arrange to have the check disappear. We'd finish the meal, finish our conversation, whether it was about their banking, their forthcoming trip up the Nile, or whatever, and then I'd say, "Well, thanks so much for joining us. I do hope you enjoyed the meal..." and rise. It never failed to impress even the wealthiest. I had, of course, arranged beforehand with the maître d' to have 20 percent for service added to the bill, another 5 percent for the captain, and the whole thing sent to me at the bank.

Having good relationships with restaurants was also helpful with clients who were partial to the big lunch— and I mean big, like one to five P.M. Those folks who were fond of champagne at lunch, and lots of other good wine, could not be rushed. Thankfully, such sessions were not too common, even though I nearly always extracted additional business for the bank at such marathons. But I'm not built for that line of work on a steady basis. When they occurred, we needed a most sympathetic maître d' and staff, the kind of service you might not find in every restaurant in town.

Many of our richest clients don't like to come into the bank. If they don't have a chauffeur or a personal secretary to do their banking for them, we go to them.

Of course, their banking needs are different to start with. No worry about Friday lines for them. If they need some cash, or want to make a deposit, we'll do it by messenger.

Rich folk don't carry or need much cash, anyway. Either they have credit cards, like normal folk, or they have personal charges at various stores they frequent. Or, they always have someone around who carries cash.

President Kennedy was famous for never carrying cash, and that was long before he became President. And England's Prince Charles was once asked by David Frost, in a famous interview, how much money he had on him. Astonished and amused, Charles reached into his pocket and came up with nothing. But then, he is never alone, and someone on his staff always has cash to cover whatever might be needed.

Though I can't think of much the Prince would need it for. Charles, like most famous rich people, can sign for pretty much anything, anywhere in the world. I knew a fellow who once worked for Huntington Hartford. Hartford signed for everything, everywhere, scribbling the address of his personal business office under the signature. The bill was to be sent there. The fellow told me he had never ever seen the signature questioned. Even, once when they had sailed on Hartford's yacht to Morocco and took dinner in some little smelly cafe in the Casbah. "Cushions, and all of us eating with our hands, that kind of place. I reached for the check, partly because it seemed the decent thing to do—it was his 120-foot yacht, after all—and partly because I knew they'd laugh at his signature in a dump like that. But, he insisted, as usual. He was a generous man in many ways. I shrugged and gave him the check; he signed it. I figured after the waiter brought it back, then I'd be able to pay. But the waiter went off, had a brief conference with a guy in a fez, and that was that. Months later, the greasy bill, that same check, arrived at his office on Lexington Avenue, and, of course, it was promptly paid."

Checklist:

The very special efforts we make for our most favored rich folk

1. No bounced checks.
2. Preferred loan treatment: Better rates, better and more flexible repayment schedules.
3. Investment advice and services.
4. Free financial advice and estate planning.
5. Introductions to other banks, lawyers, and other professionals—even real estate brokers.
6. Genuine personal service.
7. Wooing services: limos, lunches, and hot tickets.

Chapter 14

Special treatment: What you can get for yourself and your business

It ought to be clear by now that while it is certainly true that bankers can be snobs, these days, they are more interested in making money than in being genteel.

They know that everyone in the world is not Mrs. Aspinwall. They know that money is money.

To attract the rest of the world, they have concocted a whole slew of "special treatment" types of services. These mimic the special treatment they give the Mrs. Aspinwalls, and sometimes they charge you a small fee for them, instead of giving them for free as they do to Mrs. Aspinwall. Of course, they more than make up those fees from her in other ways.

Let's consider four of these service areas and see exactly what's available to you, starting with the whole business of bouncing checks.

Overdrafts

Traditionally everyone's worst fear; today, no worries. Practically every commercial bank in America today has some kind of overdraft checking system.

In our bank, we call it Convenience Credit. At Chase, they call it Overdraft Checking. At The Bank of California, it's Money Check.

The names vary; the idea is the same. What we're all doing is making you a loan today for use whenever you want to use it, sometime in the future. You fill out the form that gives us the same information as a loan application, we do the usual credit check, and if everything is okay, we make the loan to you, in the abstract. You might call it a personal line of credit.

Usually these loans run from $1,000 to $5,000, and you don't pay interest on them until you actually start to use the money.

No money changes hands. We tell the computer, extend Ms. Dougherty's regular checking account by $2,500 (or whatever) if she gets to the end of the line with her own money, wants more, and writes a check to get it. Don't bounce that check, computer. No, no.

We all charge the normal interest rates on whatever amount you actually use, and usually, you can pay us back that amount in a variety of ways. Most commonly, people have us take a regular amount from their checking account each month. Some people prefer to pay these overdraft loans off quickly. They come in a few weeks or months after they've used their $2,500, and make a deposit against that for, say, $2,000. By doing so, they replenish their overdraft well. They have $2,000 more in their overdraft credit, against which they can write more checks. On and on.

No one should be without this service. If you use overdraft credit with a bit of restraint, you probably should never again have to worry about bouncing a check.

Free investment advice

Any bank of any size maintains quite an impressive array of investment research facilities, analysts, economists, investment specialists, whom you never see.

You can gain access to some of your bank's data and intelligence, crystal balls, and the wise people who stare into them divining the future by asking for it from your bank officer.

Of course, if you've got only a few thousand dollars to invest, the amount and quality of information and guidance you receive is obviously going to be less than what Mrs. Aspinwall receives.

You might get some good advice on the best short-term investment for your $5,000. Mrs. Aspinwall, who wants to see her millions working over a three-year stretch, as opposed to your three-month killing, is going to have me talking to her about where we think interest rates will be moving, where the bond market is going, what forces are acting on it, what our economists can see happening to our economy at large, and how it will affect the investments in her multimillion buck portfolio.

Still, the limited guidance you can get for yourself can make as much difference to you as it does to Mrs. Aspinwall. And the quality of it will be good, in my opinion, just as good as the average stockbroker is going to give you, perhaps better.

Unlike stockbrokers, we don't work on a commission basis. We charge a flat fee for managing portfolios, planning them, advising, placing orders. Three quarters of 1 percent is typical. So it doesn't matter to us whether we turn your or Mrs. Aspinwall's millions over daily or let them sit for months and months. All that matters is that we do a good job, because our fee is based on the market value of the portfolio. We guess wrong, the value goes down and so does our fee. We divine correctly, value rises, pulling our nice fee along with it. Just dessert, we like to think.

Free estate planning

Any good and smart bank will give you this one at no charge, and happily so.

I said earlier that we especially love to do it for the rich because it puts us at the heart of their financial lives and much of the planning for those lives.

The same principle applies to everyone. We want to help the young hustling ad man, the divorced mother of two who is back in the marketplace again pushing real estate, the middle-level worker without a giant salary, who nevertheless knows he's got to think about tomorrow.

Estate planning is a pompous name for long-range financial perspective. Such a pompous name, in fact, that it scares away most people who aren't terribly rich. They figure, well, I don't have an estate.

But the elements of estate planning are in fact meaningful to them, as well. Do they have enough insurance? Or too much? Are they taking advantage of all possible retirement plans? If they die tomorrow, what shape will their family be in? Do they have a will? When was it last reviewed? Does it take full advantage of the latest tax laws? If they die tomorrow, will their estate be paying more taxes than is necessary?

Personal banking (sort of)

This one is trickier. This gets closer to the unwritten but important personal service we give the rich, but in truth, while we have adjusted somewhat, we still won't give true personal banking to everyone.

The term "personal banking" has come into great vogue in the last six to seven years. It came about because we all did our marketing studies, and surveys, and we all learned the same things. People in general perceived bankers as quite professional, but aloof and arrogant. They had no real contact with us, no communication; everything was terribly impersonal. Suddenly, your TV screen was full of those ads telling you how warm we really could be.

For most people, nothing much changed. There was, however, a new kind of service created for certain kinds of people, people who aren't rich, but still a financial cut above the man in the street. Not the Special Checking person, but the person making, say, $35,000 to $50,000 and up.

These people we began to entice into our banks with the promise of real personal attention. Often, we'd ask them to maintain minimum balances in their checking accounts, two to five thousand dollars, though if they dropped below those amounts, nobody much cared. The potential was still there.

These people had no lines to contend with. And they got a fair amount of investment advice, certainly lots of estate planning. They could also get us to help them out. If they needed loans, their terms might not be so good as a real richie would get, but better than most other people got. And they had a bank officer to turn to who was truly familiar with their financial affairs, who would really put together the best loan arrangement he could, and who would do it all quite fast.

We wouldn't give them tickets to the World Series, but we would certainly take them to lunch in the bank's dining room and listen to their money and banking questions and answer as best we could. If they called needing something retrieved from that dreadful micro-film pit, we would get the job done, quickly.

Even though they weren't Mrs. Aspinwall, we took the pain out of banking for them. And we still do. It's a kind of banking that might have been conceived for public relations and the shaky reasons of brightening our dour image, but we all quickly realized that this was smart banking business.

Beyond those four service areas for individuals, there are a number of other things that businesses can get from us.

1. Special treatment for your employees.

If you have an employee who needs a loan, and you do corporate business with us, give us a call. We want to keep you happy, and if bending over backwards to give a loan to your foreman or your office manager is going to make them happy and ever more loyal to you—which is going to make you happy—glad to oblige.

2. Management services, like the "notification of balance" service.

We give you a call around eleven in the morning and tell you what your balance is at that moment in your company's account. You hear the number and flash through your mind the amount you're going to be drawing down from that account for the day's business. Maybe you've got a balance of $100,000, but you know that for two days, you'll have no extraordinary expenses, no payroll for three days, so you tell us, "Okay, that's good. Invest all but, say, $25,000 in the money market fund, and let's make a few bucks in the next forty-eight hours."

We arrange it for you, moving the money out of the account. The loss to us of not having the money to invest ourselves is worth the good will we gain. We'll make the dollars back when we lend you a million dollars for your new machinery, a million, that is, at 17 percent.

3. Payrolls.

Our computers are programmed to handle our own payroll. They take all the deductions for taxes, social security, pension, insurance, and punch out the checks. Clean, efficient, and so much less expensive than doing it by hand.

Small businesses often can't afford a computer operation like that. There are private companies that offer such services, but their fees can be a bit steep. When we like a small business, we offer to do their payroll for them at a much smaller fee than a private company charges.

4. Real estate rents.

Again our computers are set up for this job. They are programmed to send out monthly bills for our loans. It's a simple matter to have them send out more monthly notices, but these are for rents due to a customer in the real estate business.

The fee is minimal here because the cash flow created by the service is so juicy. In fact, banks compete for the honor of providing this service to real estate moguls. And I have heard of banks selling the service on the basis of computer systems that didn't exist. They claimed they did, to get the business and the cash flowing in. But when billing time came, some poor secretary was typing out each and every rent bill. Still, it was worth it to the bank.

5. Relocation.

If you're going to move your business out of the dreadful, filthy city to some idyllic, suburban industrial park, your bank can be enormously helpful. In fact, before committing yourself, talk to them.

They can put you together with the best real estate brokers. Sometimes, they might even have a customer in that suburb who wants to rent space, and they can put you two together without any broker or broker's fee.

Obviously, if you are going to need a new bank, they can guide you there.

But in more subtle and important ways they can be valuable. Perhaps you are considering two different new locations, and one of the deciding factors will be the kind of labor you can find in each. You could hire a company to do a costly survey for you, or you could get that reading from your bank for nothing. If they have a branch in the new area you're considering, they'll put you with the appropriate manager. In one lunch, he can tell you enough about the kind of labor supply in those parts to settle your mind. It's his job to know the nature of the people in his community.

6. Foreign contacts.

If you have a hint that there are business possibilities for you abroad, your banker can be extremely valuable in helping you explore that new world, foreign to you in all ways.

You know that some competitors in the handbag and luggage business have been buying leather materials in Brazil, having the goods put together there for very little. But Brazil is a very, very big country, and all you know about it is Carmen Miranda, Carnival, and the names of your competitors' suppliers.

Your banker in the United States can put you together with their correspondent bank in Rio. If your man here really cares about your business, he'll do more than send a letter. He'll call the guy in Rio. "I'm about to send you a letter of introduction, Sergio, for one of our Preferred Customers, but I just wanted to have this chance to tell you a bit about him personally. You'll want to do your own credit checks, of course, make your own decision, but this man's got a very promising luggage and handbag business, he's built it very intelligently, and I think the business he wants to do in Brazil could be a very good shot for you people. So, after you get my letter and meet the guy—he'll be coming down in ten days—and have a chance to do your own homework, if you want to speak to me further, I've been given permission to talk to you..."

This last phrase, "I've been given permission to talk to you," means that your banker is willing to answer any question Sergio might come up with, to provide him with all the insights gained over some years of business.

An introduction like that will get Sergio working for you. He will introduce you to the business people he knows, who can make your new venture successful.

And since Sergio is their banker, they know that he has checked you out, before sending you to them.

7. "Lock box" accounts.

These are special techniques for processing the receipts and disbursements of corporate accounts.

Our special service with this one is really special, and not very well known. We advise companies and corporations who keep "lock box" accounts with us on the U.S. postal system.

Though the system, as we all know too well, is uniformly bad, it is worse in some parts of the country than others.

And, as anyone who has ever paid a bill knows, the slower the mail service, the better. If you can count on your trusted mailman to stumble around in sleet and snow for a week or so with your check to American Express, imagine what such a delay means to American Express. It means your $376.89 multiplied by millions.

That's the reason they give you an envelope along with your bill, and on the envelope is the address of a strange post office: strange to you because in the first place it's a post office and not the American Express office; strange in the second place because it's a kind of out-of-the-way post office. If you're in New York City and paying Amex, their envelope says, P.O. Box 1270, Newark, New Jersey 07101. Why do they want my money going to a dump like Newark, you wonder?

They don't wonder. They know that while Newark might be a dump, it has one of the most efficient post offices in the East. In fact, by having you send your check there, they will get your money two or three days faster than any other place in the world. Two or three days for the use of millions of checks means millions of dollars to Amex. To them, to a company like General Motors Acceptance Corporation, waiting for its millions of monthly car payments, even the difference of an hour can be staggering.

They know about Newark and all the other speedy post offices because they survey and monitor post offices all over America, shifting their boxes from one to another. It's well worth the cost to them.

As you might have guessed they also know which post offices are slowest. They use those outstanding stations to mail their checks from.

Not every business is American Express and can find

out when Seattle is best, Fayetteville worst. But a good bank can help them find out, and we do.

Here is a list of the best and worst post offices, as of early 1982. Maybe you can set up your own "lock box" operation.

The Best	*The Worst*
Newark, N.J.	New York City, midtown and anything
Pittsburgh, Pa.	serviced by LaGuardia and Kennedy
St. Louis, Mo.	airports
Dallas, Tex.	Chicago, Ill.
	Atlanta, Ga.

Checklist:

The Special Treatment services you can get for yourself.

1. Overdraft checking, no more bounced checks.
2. Free investment advice.
3. Free estate planning.
4. Personal banking (sort of).

Checklist:

The special services you can get for your business.

1. Special attention for your employees.
2. Management services, e.g., "notification of balance."
3. Handling payrolls.
4. Collecting real estate rents.
5. Relocation advice.
6. Providing foreign contacts.
7. "Lock box" accounts.

Chapter 15

Picking the right bank

Picking the bank that's right for you has a lot to do with attitude. If, after everything I've tried to convey in this book, you still are willing to have your bank ignore you, do you a favor to take your money, then obviously it doesn't matter where you bank.

If, on the other hand, my advice makes sense and you really do intend to change your relationship with your bank and get them to start treating you like an individual who requires particular services, then you have to find a bank that will be responsive.

Basically, as we have seen, all banks trade in the same two elements—the commodity of money and human service. So in that sense, what you have always thought—that all banks are alike—is correct. But they don't all offer their "products" in the same way.

Finding the right place for yourself should start with the bank you now use. Long-term relationships matter greatly to bankers. They don't like "walk-ins" or "bouncers," we know, and they don't like to lend money to strangers. So, if possible, stay where you are.

That is assuming they really want you, on your terms. Test them. Find out who the bank officer is who is responsible for your account and make the call I discussed in Chapter 5. See if he or she even wants you to come in for a chat and review of your affairs. If they don't, or they give you an appointment but seem dismissive and uninterested, that's all you need to know. You're going elsewhere. Using the system sketched out in Chapter 4, pursue a lead from a friend or through your company, and try to find a bank and a banker you feel wants you and your business.

The truth is that bankers need you much more than you need them, and that is the attitude you should maintain as you shop around. You are offering them the possibility of business, present and future. If they don't recognize that, you don't want to give them your business.

You might end up with a bank that is not a block away from your office. If you want service, you might have to trade off convenience, and I'd make that trade without hesitation. So many people pick a bank simply because it's close to them, forever moan about the way they are treated, and are too lazy to take their business elsewhere.

In your search, be thinking long term. Like finding a business partner, you want someone you can work with for many years.

If you decide to leave your present bank for good reasons, probably the best place for you to look first is your company's bank, going in with a recommendation, as I suggested. For most people, that's how to start off with the most clout. One important tip: Be sure you go to the very branch where the company maintains its accounts. That's where the company's business matters. Branches are competitive. If you go to a different branch, a bank officer might be aware that your company is a client, but it won't mean much to him. His branch manager won't be telling him to be certain to give extra attention to anyone from the Giant Products

Corporation because all that business and the credit for it is going to a rival branch manager.

Often you will find that your choice will be a decision between convenience and service. All my advice notwithstanding, you have to satisfy your own needs. Perhaps you're all over town, need cash at odd hours. Maybe you must have one of the largest banks in your city that offers you branches everywhere and money machines too.

Those are not the banks, however, where you will get much of any service. They are geared to volume, period. Go into some of these banks today, and you don't find any real bank officers. There is no one with any authority to do anything. All they have are glorified tellers who can punch terminals and tell you what your balance is. Those banks simply don't hire people to give you service of the sort we've been discussing.

Is it not possible to have the best of both worlds? Many people keep two accounts: a minimal balance in one of the giant banks, so they can always get from a cash machine, the $50 emergency money they need on a weekend; and a much larger account with the bank where they expect personal service.

If you do that, don't confuse the function and purpose of each bank. One is a cash machine, the other is a bank. Don't bother developing any kind of relationship with the money machine people. Waste of your time.

If you're a commuter, with your business in the big city, you very well might want to maintain a small account in a local bank near your home. This is an exception to my basic rule of keeping all your accounts in one bank to get the most clout. Still, a lot of people have told me how helpful it is to maintain that local account for household expenses only. It's a way to keep those matters apart from others and to avoid hassles with local merchants when they go to cash checks.

That local account, no matter how modest, can also represent an important second source of credit. Local banks are always trying to lure more and more of your business away from the big downtown places, and often they will lend you money on better terms than you can find downtown.

When money is tight, local banks will lend only to their own customers. That small account you have makes you a customer, and it could give you an important new opportunity for a loan.

If through your search you bear in mind Cook's Law—*banks need you more than you need them*—you'll settle with the bank that is best for you. And then you will, probably for the first time in your life, see a bank work for you, rather than the other way around.

APPENDIX

If you have a problem or complaint over the treatment you're receiving from any bank, credit agency, loan company, collection agency, or any store or credit card company, here's where to call or write.

First, call your state's attorney general's office. Vigilance in this area of consumer life varies from state to state, but the great majority now are tough, move quickly, often supported by state laws that are as strong as the federal acts.

However, if you don't find satisfaction there, go federal. If your dispute is with a bank, contact one of the following.

If the bank is nationally chartered ("National" or "N.A." will appear in the bank's name), write to: Comptroller of the Currency, Consumer Affairs Division, Washington, D.C. 20219

- If the bank is state chartered and is a member of the Federal Reserve System, write to: Board of Governors of the Federal Reserve System, Director, Division of Consumer Affairs, Washington, D.C. 20551

- If the bank is state chartered and is insured by the Federal Deposit Insurance Corporation (FDIC) but is not a member of the Federal Reserve System, write to: Federal Deposit Insurance Corporation, Office of Bank Customer Affairs, Washington, D.C. 20429

- If a federally chartered or federally insured savings and loan association is involved, write to: Federal Home Loan Bank Board, Washington, D.C. 20552

- If a federally chartered credit union is involved, write to: Federal Credit Union Administration, Division of Consumer Affairs, Washington, D.C. 20456

If your trouble comes from one of the other financial or credit organizations, or stores or companies, contact the Federal Trade Commission, Washington, D.C. 20580, or one of the FTC regional offices:

- ATLANTA REGIONAL OFFICE: 1718 Peachtree Street, N.W., Suite 1000, Atlanta, Georgia 30309

- BOSTON REGIONAL OFFICE: 1301 Analex Building, 150 Causeway, Boston, Massachusetts 02114

- CHICAGO REGIONAL OFFICE: Suite 1437, 55 East Monroe Street, Chicago, Illinois 60603

- CLEVELAND REGIONAL OFFICE: Suite 500, The Mall Bldg., 118 Saint Clair, Cleveland, Ohio 44114

- SAN FRANCISCO REGIONAL OFFICE: 450 Golden Gate Avenue, Box 36005, San Francisco, California 94102

- DALLAS REGIONAL OFFICE: 2001 Bryan Street, Suite 2665, Dallas, Texas 75201

- DENVER REGIONAL OFFICE: Suite 2900, 1405 Curtis Street, Denver, Colorado 80202

- LOS ANGELES REGIONAL OFFICE: 11000 Wilshire Blvd., Room 13209, Los Angeles, California 90024

- NEW YORK REGIONAL OFFICE: 22nd Floor, Federal Bldg., 26 Federal Plaza, New York, New York, 10007

- SEATTLE REGIONAL OFFICE: 28th Floor, Federal Bldg., 915 Second Ave., Seattle, Washington 98174

If your trouble is with a collection company, representing a bank or any of the other companies mentioned above, make your complaint to the agency that governs the bank or company that hired that collection company just as they are listed above.

Index

251

ABOUT THE AUTHORS

JOHN A. COOK has been in banking for over seventeen years, most of that time with The Bank of New York, briefly with Manufacturers Hanover Bank.

His experience included consumer banking, being a loan officer and group head at The Bank of New York's largest branch; managing trusts; developing and selling bank services to other financial institutions.

He was a vice-president of The Bank of New York when he left in 1981 to write this book and develop business ventures of his own.

ROBERT WOOL is the coauthor of *All You Need to Know About the IRS*, which was a national best seller in two separate editions.

He is president of Premier Cru Books, Inc., his New York book packaging company, which produced this book and is creating others for several publishers.

Before starting his book packaging company, he was political editor of *The New York Times Magazine*, executive editor of *New York Magazine*, editor in chief of *The Washington Post Magazine*, and founder and editor in chief of *Show Magazine*. As a writer, he has contributed to *Esquire*, *Playboy*, *Atlantic*, and *The New York Times* among other magazines, and published one novel.

He lives in New York with his wife, Bridget Potter, and their daughter, Vanessa.

MONEY TALKS!
How to get it and How to keep it!

☐	23716	I.B.M. COLOSSUS IN TRANSITION by Robert Sobel	$4.95
☐	23586	BERNARD MELTZER SOLVES YOUR MONEY PROBLEMS by Bernard Meltzer	$3.95
☐	23489	SALARY STRATEGIES by Marilyn Moats Kennedy	$3.50
☐	23913	ALL YOU NEED TO KNOW ABOUT BANKS by John Cook & Robert Wool	$3.95
☐	23568	GET A JOB IN 60 SECONDS by Steve Kravette	$2.95
☐	22850	MONEYWISE by Mimi Brien	$3.50
☐	22509	THE BOOK OF FIVE RINGS by Miyamoto Musashi	$2.95
☐	22936	HOW TO GET FREE TAX HELP by Matthew Lesko	$2.95
☐	23455	YOU CAN NEGOTIATE ANYTHING by Herb Cohen	$3.95
☐	24138	GUERRILLA TACTICS IN THE JOB MARKET by T. Jackson	$3.95
☐	23563	THE ONLY INVESTMENT GUIDE YOU'LL EVER NEED by Andrew Tobias	$3.95
☐	23453	HOW TO WAKE UP THE FINANCIAL GENIUS INSIDE YOU by Mark Oliver Haroldsen	$3.50
☐	20296	THE COMING CURRENCY COLLAPSE: And What You Can Do About It.	$3.95
☐	20478	THE COMPLETE BOOK OF HOME BUYING by M. Sumichrast & R. Shafer	$3.95
☐	23099	THE GAMESMAN: The New Corporate Leaders by Michael Maccoby	$3.95
☐	22909	THE GREATEST SALESMAN IN THE WORLD by Og Mandino	$2.75
☐	22550	ALMOST EVERYONE'S GUIDE TO ECONOMICS by Galbraith/Salinge	$2.95
☐	20191	HIGH FINANCE ON A LOW BUDGET by Mark Skousen	$2.95

Prices and availability subject to change without notice.